Aging with Humor and Grace

A Hilarious Woman's Guide Using Funny Stories and Embarrassing Moments as Milestones in Life's Journey

Andrea Partee

Copyright © 2013 Andrea Partee
Second Edition 2014
Front Cover Art by Sharon Krock
All rights reserved.

ISBN-13:978-1484991688

ISBN-10:1484991680

DEDICATION

This book is dedicated to …**laughter**. It lightens the load and cures what ails. As it turns out even the roughest of times can be funny.

A big thank you to my friend Sandra King for all her help, support and encouragement which was occasionally disguised as pushing, prodding and lecturing. (I'm going to hear about this.)

To my long time friend and naturopath, Debra MacIntyre Kviesis; for her love, healing, support and friendship. I still laugh when I remember her telling me I was going through menopause and I almost jumped down her throat with denial.

And to my ex mother-in-law Betty who swore I was funnier than Erma Bombeck.

I love you all very much.

CONTENTS

Book One - Body Parts

	Introduction	i
1	Let's Start at the Top	1
2	Well Slap My Forehead, Aging Starts Here	2
3	No One Over Thirty Knows Their Hair Color Right?	5
4	Eyebrows - Where Oh Where Can They Be?	15
5	Eyes and When Cucumbers are for More Than Eating	19
6	The Nose - Why Don't Boobs Keep Growing Instead?	29
7	I Missed Tongue Day at Insecurity School	33
8	Who Stole my Lips?	35
9	Teeth Improve Your Smile	40
10	Ears - When Cleaning and Ironing Don't Work	55
11	Wasn't it Supposed to be One Chin Per Neck?	57
12	Boobs, the Fraternal Twins	59
13	Stomachs - Why Have a Flat One Anyway?	66
14	History of an Ass	68
15	Legs Make You Taller	74
16	Feet and Piggly Wigglies	83

Book Two - Life's Little Experiences

17	Bodily Functions	88
18	Female Fashions – If It's Not Comfortable, Wear It	101
19	Body Hair and the Great Migration	111
20	Moles, Freckles and Liver Whats?	116
21	Dumb Shit	120
22	Pregnancy	126
23	Raising Kids	130
24	The Snap, Crackle and Pop of Exercise	134
24	The Highs and Lows, Hot and Colds of Menopause	148
26	Am I Grown Up Yet?	152
	About the Author	154

INTRODUCTION

Before we begin, let's go down memory lane for just a minute to give us perspective.

Remember how eager we were to grow up and do whatever we wanted and then found out that was a bunch of bull?

Kids have to answer to their parents and teachers, without realizing they will have to listen to someone far worse as adults. Themselves! Boy can we be hard on ourselves can't we?

Some years ago I made an effort to teach a couple of five-year-olds gratitude for their tender young age.

My sons were three and five years old and I babysat two boys the same ages, five days a week.

Once on a trip to the grocery store, the two eldest started whining about having the short end of the stick because they were kids.

First they were annoyed I made everyone hold hands to get from the car to the store entrance. We got a lot of stares walking 5 wide.

As we entered, their comments flowed. When they were grown they were going to buy whatever they wanted; go wherever they wanted and do whatever they wanted.

Finally my eldest babysittee, Jason blurted, "I wanna be the adult right now!"

"That works for me," I said. "First we need to finish the shopping. If you want to help me climb into the shopping cart, I'll give you the list and you can get everything.

Be sure to add it all up in your head so there's enough money when we get to checkout. It's so embarrassing to not have enough money."

"Let's see," I continued, "When we get home, you can put away the groceries, and make the tuna sandwiches for lunch. Afterward, read a nap time story for the two little ones."

"Then can we play?" Jason asked.

"No! The kitchen must be cleaned, the dog has to go potty and the clothes need to be washed, dried, folded and put away."

"Then can we play?" Jason asked.

I don't know. How does the play room look? Did you guys put the toys away before we came to the store?"

"No. After we do that, can we play?" Jason queried beginning to sound disappointed.

If you hurry you might get in ten minutes because it will probably be time to start dinner.

"Maybe I don't want to be an adult yet."

"I know. Me either," I agreed, "Tell ya what though. If you guys help me with the chores I bet we'll have time to go to the park before you go home."

"You got a deal!"

* * *

Each age and each stage has its blessings. I hope you are enjoying wherever you are in life.

As for myself, I am finally old enough to do what I want.

I can laugh at myself... and do my best to stick around and enjoy life... wrinkles and all.

Book One

~*~

Body Parts

Why Wrinkle Eraser and Collagen Could
Save the Day

1

Let's Start from the Top

The first thing we notice is the aging of our face.

You know, those sneaky little wrinkles that flair out from our eyes like star shine and the half circles at each end of our mouth that remind us of a caricature?

That's nothing. If that's all you have at this point, you haven't lived! And while you're paying attention to your face, your boobs are falling, your knees are rearranging and cottage cheese is taking over your thighs.

If you happen to be a man reading this; laugh all you want because you, my dear, while watching your wife develop ski slopes on her chest or teasing her about accidentally tucking her breasts into her waistband are growing the boobs she once had. Go ahead, lift up your shirt and take a look. See?

2

Well Slap my Forehead, Aging Starts Here

Slapping the forehead does not flatten wrinkles. If I'd known having facial expressions caused forehead creases, I would have stopped having emotions long ago.

Between slapping my forehead for having kids and raising my eyebrows in response to kids, I wore the poor thing out. After all, giving out the mom look takes its toll.

You know, the subtle one where you tilt your head down at a very slight angle, raise your eyebrows high enough that your forehead resembles a Shar Pei puppy. Hold that look for several seconds and they KNOW if they don't cease and desist whatever they're doing the shit is going to hit the fan. It's worked for eons.

In retrospect, I should have made them put part of their allowance in the jar each time they got the mom look. I'd have enough saved for a facelift by now.

Wow, I just figured something out. Using the look begins when a child is about 3-years-old. You took three seconds to pee, walk into the kitchen only to find the little bugger has dragged a chair to the counter; climbed up and is in the cabinet stuffing his face full of cookies. No need to yell, the look says it all.

Here's the math, assuming your kids leave home at 18 (bah-ha-ha-ha) and you've only had to use the look twice a day per kid. Mine goes like this:

$$2 \text{ times a day} \times 16 \text{ years} \times 356 \text{ days} = 11{,}392$$

$$11{,}392 \times 3 \text{ kids} = 34{,}176$$

Add nieces, nephews, friends kids, and your kids' best friends who live at your house and the numbers climb.

Don't forget kids at the park, skating rink, movie theater, arcade, mall, McDonalds indoor playground, school (because you volunteer), and Six Flags for those who cut in line. Over the course of 18 years, the total soars to:

$$642{,}891$$

If your kids live at home till they're 22, there is added tension and frustration, plus the goobers think they are adults. This raises the total to:

$$1{,}496{,}211$$

As if that wasn't enough. You got so used to using the look, that your husband, the cat, both dogs and the ferret also experience your wrath.

Since spouses don't listen any better than the kids or the dogs, the total has just skyrocketed to:

2,011,006

(The ferret is hiding inside the couch cushion and you haven't seen him in two days.) I may have missed a few because here's what happened on Tuesday while talking to my son on the phone.

"Mom, are you giving me the look?"

"No honey (eek). You're 25, married and all grown up. You are an adult who makes his own decisions."

"Mom, I can feel it. You are giving me the look."

"I'm so sorry honey. Old habits die hard. Does it still work?"

"Damn it yes! I hate it! (Pause) ...But the puppy hasn't peed on the floor since last Sunday when you were here and gave him the look, so I appreciate that one."

(Snicker, snicker. That's the power of motherhood.)

Shit, I just realized if I'd collected bits of their allowance, I would own a Mercedes to go with that facelift. Hindsight!

Hiding the Shar Pei Forehead

I cut bangs when I was 45. Never had them in my life but then I had never had wrinkles on my forehead either. This was a first attempt at dealing with the aging process.

Twelve years later I lifted my bangs to see how it was going under there and by god my forehead now looks younger than the rest of my face!

I'm growing out my bangs. I could never keep the darn things straight anyway.

3

No One Over 30 Knows Their Hair Color Right?

Heck, I'm not sure anyone over the age of twelve knows their real hair color anymore since changing hair color is as common as changing your shoes.

I've never gone with hot pink or bright blue hair but I have colored, highlighted and low lighted in shades close to *someone's* natural color.

Why is it, when hair begins to turn gray it starts the little internal clock ticking? The fear clock, reminding us we're getting closer to check-out time.

I never worried about gray hair until the past year and I'm blaming everyone but me.

I have a *lot* of gray, but I still have a full head of the stuff. And I don't necessarily relate gray to old since my mom was gray when I was born. At 30, I was her fourth bundle of joy.

I was a surprise baby. A prophylactic pregnancy or, rubber baby as I smilingly call myself. Maybe her gray came with me. All I know for sure is they really couldn't afford me, but they made it work. My bassinet was a dresser drawer.

Dad got his first gray hair in his mid fifties and I staved off the boring color until a surgery at 40. I guess getting that tumor out of my face stressed me out because overnight several big white hairs appeared.

Being totally proud of my mature color, I plucked them. This made them reproduce at an alarming rate, plus it hurt! I moved on to cutting them off for awhile until I got used to them.

Then me, myself and I decided "What the heck! It's natural so let's just go with it." This worked for a few years until my friends started bugging me.

Here are a few lines I heard often, followed by what I was thinking:

- "Did you *know* you have gray hairs?" (No, do I? My mirror shattered in the summer of '89.)

- "How can you *stand* that gray?" (You pay for highlights; I've got the salt and pepper look for free)

- "You *need* to color your hair!" (Why? You have a nice color but it looks like straw and I think it's thinning.)

- "Girlfriend, its *time* you do something about *that* - dye your hair!" (You think I should go blonde?)

So much for friends! I acquiesced eventually and changed from dark brown to dark red. This wasn't exactly a personal choice.

I just wanted my dark brown; but what I learned about

doing self color is, no matter what color I used, it came out a shade of red. Even with L'Oreal (and I deserved it.)

Black was the only exception. Lucky me! The plan was to use black and it would fade to brown so I didn't have red. Black made me feel gothic and it made my skin look washed out. Not easy for someone of olive complexion.

After the black fiasco, I decided I loved red. It only cost eight bucks.

When it got to the point I needed two hair coloring kits at a time for my long hair, I decided to go natural.

It's not just that I'm cheap (even though I could probably give Scrooge a run for his money), it's that the hair color was ruining my hair and I thought thick gray and silver would be better than dry breaking thin red brown hair.

Plus, it's a pain in the butt to get hair color off the sink, the counters, the kitchen floor or the toilet.

A year later, the line between the silver/gray and red was faded and nearly to my shoulders. I thought the colors pretty. What should happen next? A friend struck again.

"You *are* going to color your hair before your son's wedding aren't' you? It'll make you look years younger." (Slouch)

Shit. I just don't see how coloring my hair is going to make my wrinkles look less noticeable. I am who I am. I am 57 years young. You'd think I'd be old enough to not buy into all this stuff.

Barbie dolls don't have realistic figures. Models don't have realistic figures and I have yet to look younger and have shinier, silkier hair from hair color, no matter what the commercials promise.

So did I buy into the BS? Me?

Come on, my ex would be there along with my kids' step mother. Not only did I buy into it, I actually paid someone to do it right.

Haircuts and Hair Styles

My two hair fears are...

One, a color shade so dark it makes a woman look *older*. You know what I mean? The skin looks pale, the wrinkles deeper and you get the impression the gal thinks she's still 35 when she's going on 65.

And two, having the same style one had in high school. Why do women do this? Instead of hiding their age, they're shouting it out with a megaphone. Change isn't easy but sometimes you have to be courageous.

My Own Hairstyle

You may have to remind me of the second one when you see me because I am guilty, guilty, guilty! The truth is I will never be fashionable.

My excuse is that I have had long hair most my life and I get compliments on it still. It may be that my hair is pretty but not *on me*. Who knows?

And my number one reason for keeping my long hair is my Yaya (Grandmother).

My Yaya was the most wonderful being on earth; and she had long hair. She wore it in a quick low braided bun around the house and I was always in awe when she'd unpin it and brush it out. She had gray tresses to her waist and I wanted to be just like her when I grew up.

In her home she would dance with me bra-less in her

house dress, have pillow fights and laugh, laugh, laugh.

When we took a taxi to town (she never learned to drive), her hair would be piled high on her head; her lipstick perfect; her transformed breasts much higher placed than at home and her high heels, stylish.

Everyone *KNEW* her. Wherever we shopped, people called her "Mama" and I was so proud to be at her side that I swore to be just like her.

Hair Magazines

Whenever I'd look at the fashion magazines for ideas on a new hair style, it always seemed to involve cutting off 12 – 18 inches in some sort of layered style that would either cost a fortune to maintain or take years to grow out.

I saved myself time and money by keeping it grown out. At least I had options of wearing it up or down or half and half.

I'd look under long hair styles to try and update myself. Here's the problem? I don't know who pays these 'consultants' they get for magazines but they show long hair as just past the shoulders. The ends of mine sway over the toilet water when I pee.

It's like someone telling you they have a big dog when it weighs 35 pounds and you have a Great Dane tipping the scales at 135. See what I mean?

It's absolutely no help when perusing articles on holiday hair dos showing hair with a bow, a clip or a few pearls. That is *not* on my list of innovative or trendy hairdos when I can do that stuff by using my old jewelry or sticking a package bow on my head.

They may get away with it for a young skinny

magazine model, but if a 50-something year old woman does it there will be snickers behind her back wherever she goes.

Hopefully these writers will be able to find other jobs to support their drug habits. Scouring these magazines in hyper drive while waiting in a fast moving grocery store line, is hardly worth my time. (I had to hurry so I could get to the tabloids and read stories not to believe.)

Can you imagine how angry I'd be if I'd actually paid for one of those rags?

My Daughter's Hair

My teenage daughter is half me and half her dad. She doesn't buy magazines either. She does free searches on the internet. That's as far as her thriftiness goes.

She prints a picture of the newest hairstyle that's going to make her look fabulous and takes it to the salon. She gets the cut of her dreams and her father pays.

Mind you, she has thick, heavy, wavy hair to die for… so she has it thinned, layered and uses a hair straightener every day. And every time she gets a new style, she loves it… for a week; and then vows to grow it back out to her waist.

Never happens.

My girl isn't unique. I've noticed those who don't succumb to the style of the hour in their teen years, cut their tresses off for good after they get married in their 20's. Why?

Others seemed to think having a baby was the definitive time to whack off the locks. Rarely did the women I knew look particularly good unless they spent an hour in the bathroom each day with hot rollers, curling iron, hair straightener, mouse', hair spray and volumizer.

Who's got time for that stuff with a baby?! These same women told me they didn't see how I kept my hair long because it was so much work.

How much work is it to wash and comb, whip it into a pony tail, a braid or a bun? Still they had me convinced I was missing something.

When I had my third and last child, I celebrated with a tubal ligation and haircut. (No rubber babies for me, even though Mom said I turned out to be a blessing.)

I went to a fancy well known salon and gave the hairdresser full reign. For an arm and a leg he whacked it off at my shoulders and pronounced it beautiful.

I thought it sucked. I couldn't believe he had a new Mercedes. So much for Buckhead (Atlanta)! I could have used the kitchen shears myself and gone out for a nice dinner.

My friends and neighbors all said it looked great but the looks on their faces did not always correspond to the words. I grew it back out.

Once it got to my waist, I decided it would be great to have it permed. That wavy look where you wash, dry and scrunch would give me volume (sorry folks, I come from the "Big Hair" era) and it would be different than my nearly straight hair.

I hemmed and hawed over who should do it for me. Turned out perming long hair is really expensive. I went with a woman who was recommended by a friend. She worked in and owned her own shop. I had a flower business at the time and her customers had great hair and everyone seemed happy with their results.

I worked a deal with the owner. I'd swap 4 gorgeous fresh flower arrangements over the course of four weeks for my waist length hair perm.

The big day arrived. I was excited. It took a long time to get it all just right before she told me to sit and wait for the magic.

While I looked at magazines knowing how beautiful I was going to look, she got on the phone and didn't look back.

It seemed a long time but what did I know? I'd never had a perm and she was a professional.

I walked out looking more like Bozo the Clown, than Andrea with gorgeous waves. I had been totally fried by chemicals.

I was not having good luck with hair. I still finished the deal, and with my last flower delivery one of the gals in the shop approached me. "Look," she whispered, "I know she fried your hair and I don't know why she didn't own up to it, but, I would be happy to cut it for you for free so you can start over. I don't know if you noticed, but it looks awful."

She gave me her card and I went out to my car and sobbed.

I knew it looked terrible but not one of my friends had the nerve to tell me I looked like something the dog dragged in.

The gal was an angel in disguise. For the first time in my life I had a pretty hair cut. It was really short for me with the longest parts almost to my shoulders.

She figured out my real hair. She layered it and the cut was so well done, all I had to do was wash, comb and scrunch.

Everyone at the office thought I'd spent hours on it. (Yes I worked and had my own business. A divorced mom has to raise her 3 kids and life should never be boring. That means no time for sleep.)

I was starting to feel pretty. A few months later after

she talked me into color and highlights I felt like a diva.

The only problem with my beautiful hair was the amount of salon visits it took to keep it up, and the vast amount money it cost along the way. What little personal time I had in my life seemed to be eaten up by my hair and the kids were getting tired of the salon as their new second home.

That's about the time I met my third and final husband. After several months he commented about my old pictures and how pretty my long hair had been and would I ever grow it out again.

We made a deal. Neither of us would cut our hair again.

I didn't mind. I thought of Yaya and smiled. And I thought of his do-it-yourself-with-$14-sheers haircuts and smiled bigger.

The time we saved on haircuts I used wisely. Two people with waist long hair can plug up a shower in about the time it takes to make a cup of Ramen noodles.

Hair and How it Affects Your Children

While my hair has had its ups, downs and colors, I don't stay bothered about what other people think. How my kids feel is an entirely different matter.

My kids and I lived in different states for awhile, seeing each other only once a year. Our relationship stayed strong keeping up over the phone.

But let me tell you, I wanted to cry when I saw the look on my son's face when we met in baggage claim at the airport. It was shock.

When I tried to talk to him about it later, he denied it but I could feel him staring at me from behind… just like

I did with my dad.

I hadn't seen Daddy in a few years and actually felt frightened when I saw his once thick black hair was now thin and totally gray. It didn't matter that he was 80, something about that color hair made me realize he wouldn't be around forever.

And even though my son swore it didn't matter, I could feel him relax when I had it colored for his brother's wedding.

4

Eyebrows - Where Oh Where Can They Be?

Eyebrows are sneaky, especially for a woman of Greek descent. In a woman's mid fifties several move south and take root above the lip to enhance our Mediterranean mustache.

While we're sulking over having to wax the mustache, the eyebrows are thinning and trying to make a full fledged escape.

We buy into the notion at an early age there is a correct shape they should be and we do our best to create and maintain that shape.

My favorite is the eye framing eyebrow with a slight arch. This is not to be confused with the arch that looks like a half circle and leaves you looking in a state of perpetual surprise, is totally unnatural, and 99% pencil.

Personally I had to do a lot of work in the eyebrow department. Being half Greek, I put Brook Shield's eyebrows to shame.

In actuality, I had one large unibrow which I began plucking at the age of twelve. Having difficulty keeping up with the mini forest above my nose, my method of control changed to shaving three months later and continues to this day (40+ years - eek.)

There was quite a bit of plucking going on as well. Thick enough to make any shape I wanted, had it been fashionable, I probably could have created two eyebrows on each side.

If I had left my eyebrows totally natural, I might have been confused with Chewie the Chewbacca from the first Star Wars movie.

My *eyebrow* and I had a truce in my 20s. I shaved the middle to make her look like twins and only plucked stragglers sneaking down my eyelids and the trailers that would have ended my eyebrows near the top of my ears. Basically there was good shape, just a lot of it.

I don't think my older sister approved of my chosen style since she seemed to make a point of plucking hers in my presence on a regular basis and offering to "fix" mine.

The older she got, the thinner her eyebrows became.

* * *

Six or seven years ago, I gained a real appreciation for what was once an unruly unibrow.

At a family get together I noticed my aunt and my sister staring at me. "What?" I said, as I approached the two sneaky relatives.

"You have eyebrows!" said my aunt Helen accusingly. Now this woman looks fabulous at 80 and since her face is not on me, I never noticed her eyebrows were gone and pencil now replaced them. My sister bemoaned, "Why do you have eyebrows and I don't?"

By now I'm feeling a little defensive. My sisters can do it to me every time. "Well," I answered, "Maybe it's because I didn't pluck them for 30 years. Remember, mine were always a bit more Brook Shield-ish."

"That's true," she answered in her condescending tone as she looked down her nose at me.

* * *

Once I got over *the look* from my sister, I had five years of eyebrow happiness.

While standing under the 400 watt bulb in the bathroom wearing my reading glasses and trimming my bangs I thought one of my head hairs was stuck to my eyebrow.

When I tried to lift it off, I realized it was a long gray eyebrow hair!

I set myself down and had a talk with me. I told me this was a normal part of life and aging and I'd better lose the attitude.

Taking my conversation seriously, I walked with pride and determination to the computer to share it with the entire world by posting it on Facebook.

My niece was gracious enough to laugh at me and tell me she hoped she looked as good as I do when she gets to be my age. I admitted in a private message that my Facebook avatar was five years old and I either had to choose whether to update it now or never.

If I didn't do it soon, maybe no one would recognize me since the eyebrow fiasco proved I was falling apart at the seams.

When our conversation was over, I went through the computer for a more recent picture. After spending two hours on a dozen pictures of myself in Photoshop (to erase just a few of the wrinkles), I felt like a fraud.

I swapped my own picture out for one of my dogs; went to the mirror and plucked the bastard out.

5

Eyes and When Cucumbers are for More Than Eating

Now I know why mature women don't wear eye makeup. I was lead to believe it was because they didn't buy into the BS. Makeup doesn't make us who we are. It's our inner beauty that counts, right?

I'm pretty sure we can all agree on that. Besides, it takes time to put a face on every day. Have we not earned the right to stop wasting our time with this stuff?

All three of my sisters believe that.

Then tell me why I see a blank canvas needing work every time I nix the makeup?

I still believe makeup has its place and it's been a ritual for a very long time. Don't hate me, but I *enjoy* the process. I like how I look with makeup and it makes me feel good about myself. It's like wearing a clean matching outfit when leaving the house instead of striped pants with a flowered shirt. Know what I mean?

Wearing eye makeup as we get older must change. I'm

beginning to think it's harder to do now than it was the first time in my teens. Here're a few little discoveries:

- One day I put my makeup on as usual. I got something in my eye and couldn't find it so I took a mirror outside with me for better light. In the full light of the sun I looked like a retired (or should-be retired) hooker and realized I desperately needed a makeover.

- Sparkly eye shadow brings attention to eyelid wrinkles making them appear like chasms in the earth's crust. If you even experiment with it, it takes 13 days to get it out of the cracks.

- Creamy eye shadow moves around even more than when we were younger. It collects in the cracks and a bright color is reminiscent of a room full of laser beams crisscrossing everywhere to protect a precious piece of art.

- Still, I'm thinking it might work like putty if I could find a color that matches my natural skin tone. Maybe covered with a powder eye shadow my eyelids would look like they use to.

- Using eyeliner can take months to get a straight line. Once you master one eye, you find the other is wrinkled completely different and needs a different technique. The only way to make it work is to keep it thin and as close to the eyelashes as possible.

- Using mascara isn't any more difficult than it used to be but now I have to lift my saggy eyelid out of the way while I put it on and blow dry it.

So why is it harder to apply makeup now? There are two separate challenges to this. The first is

Eyesight

How can you do a great makeup job when you can't see your own eyes without your glasses on? Have you ever tried reaching that little eye shadow brushy thing under your glasses to get your eyelid?

Nine times out of ten, you shadow your eyeball on the way to your eyelid. Then you must use eye drops to clear things up before you try again.

Vision is enough of a challenge without changing your eye color with a splash of shadow.

I know, I know. I hear you say I should use a 2X or 3X makeup mirror, but I do! As it turns out, I need *a lot more light* to see things than I used to.

Not wanting to blackout the entire city to put on my face, or set up a table in front of my car with the high beams on, I try to hold up my little 3X mirror closer to the light bulb with only my contact lenses in so I don't need my reading glasses …but then I don't have two free hands.

Once wrinkles have set in, one must gently flatten things out before applying anything to the eyes AND you have to know which way the wrinkle will fall back into place or your eyeliner won't match up at all. So, the second challenge is…

Getting Makeup on Between the Wrinkles

Even if you drink 37 glasses of water to stay hydrated, it does not repair the loss of elasticity in your face. That means every time you tug or stretch it creates a new wrinkle or a stretched spot that refuses to return no matter how much you plump, push, pat or beg it.

No doubt this is why so many women really give up wearing the stuff.

I'm waiting for a collagen facial spray that either puts the elasticity back or at least makes something spring back to where it was before the makeup ritual began.

I don't think that's too much to ask. I just don't see how billions of dollars have been spent on technology to make cell phones and computers smaller while wrinkles are getting bigger. Computers have not been around nearly as long as wrinkles and if mine get any bigger I'll be able to keep bus change or Laundromat money in them.

Someone needs to get their priorities straight and work on something important.

Several times I've tried to change things up. I've tried the smudged look instead of eyeliner so I don't need a straight line that turns out looking crooked because of a fold in my left eyelid.

The smudged look with wrinkles leaves me looking like a woman who just came out of hibernation with the bears. Except of course I wouldn't lose weight after not eating all winter. I have a metabolism slow as molasses.

I've tried just a bit of eye shadow and mascara and adding lipstick. The eye makeup just doesn't do quite enough. The lipstick looks good but I've never really been a lipstick wearer and it turns out I have a habit of resting my chin on my hand and rubbing my lips with my fingers when I think.

You might get away with lipstick smeared on your cheek when you're young but not at my age. I'm afraid a cop will spot me after I've been contemplating something at a red light; see the bright smear and pull me over as suspect for a DUI or driving legally blind.

Vision is Useful for Other Stuff Too

I'm a good driver. I've driven cars, trucks and buses and my vision is great during the day as long as I don't drive on a warm day with the windows down. This causes at least one contact lens to dry out, curl up and fly off, never to be seen again.

Not only does this impair my distance vision and my peripheral vision on one side but I look ridiculous driving with one eye shut. Any semi truck drivers near me mistake it for a wink and think I am flirting with them.

I imagine they think they're going to get something special at the next truck stop for a twenty spot. Who knows?

Driving in the Dark

Once the sun has set, driving becomes a totally different beast. Needing more light to see than I used to, it feels like I'm locked in a dark closet; my headlights a duo of flashlights who's batteries are exhausted.

Unless it's a road I know like the back of my hand, I avoid driving at night. Living in rural areas for many years, I'm just as afraid of hitting a deer, raccoon or possum that may appear out of nowhere, as I am of running off a road whose white line often escapes me, especially in the rain.

Talking, Texting and Driving

Not only is it illegal, it would be moronic for me to try. I know because I have.

Obviously no one can keep their entire attention on the road if talking or texting while driving a motor vehicle. If you add needing reading glasses to see the phone it goes beyond stupid.

Here's a scenario. I'm on the highway driving from one son's house to the other. Son #1 keeps texting to see when I'll be there. He worries I'm lost or may have an accident, while Son #2 is texting to see if I'll pick something up he left at Son #1's house and stop by the grocery store for eggs before I come home.

I am too polite for my own good. When the phone rings I want to answer it. When I get a text I want to read it and respond right now.

To top it off, I am still a mother who wonders if something is wrong when the little voice in my cell keeps announcing, "*Ding! Ding! Ding! You have a text message!*" I'd shoot the woman, but then I'd have to get another phone.

I get in the center lane of the three lanes, in a spot where no one is near me; whip out my reading glasses and set them low on my nose. This way I can look up and see the road clearly and look down and read a text message on a sunny day *if* I put the phone under the steering wheel between my knees.

As you can guess, this is not a smart move but I do it just long enough to know no one is bleeding and needs a ride to the hospital.

After being dumb enough to do this a few times I got

all three of my kids together, gave them *The Mom Look* while telling them NOT to text me when it's important. If anyone is bleeding; if anyone has an urgent reason to get a hold of me... call on the phone!

If I am driving I will NOT pick up the phone unless they continue to call in rapid succession because I can't even see who is calling me without my glasses and surely I do not want to renew a magazine subscription while driving 55 - 65 mph sandwiched between a semi and a couple of teenage boys playing music so loud the base is making my truck and eardrums reverberate.

How did they react? They chewed me out for ever picking up the phone while driving in the first place.

Glasses, Contacts or Both

I love my contact lenses. Wearing the kind that stay in for thirty days at a time helps me find the bathroom in the middle of the night. Also handy is the ability to see where I hid the Reese's Peanut Butter Cups at 2 am.

* * *

I never keep junk food in my bedroom. That would be too easy. If I'm going to eat something that will ruin my health, I at least have to work for it. That means getting out from under the 75 lb dog who was laying at my feet when I went to bed and is now on my legs which I didn't notice because they've been numb for hours.

Giving my legs a quick rub down so they work, the pins and needles kick in. I throw on my big wraparound robe and the warm fuzzy slippers with the Scooby Doo heads that my daughter left behind.

I shuffle down the hall because my mind is as sleepy as my legs and switch on the 25 watt light over the stove. I ponder where I hid the damn chocolate this time. I never put them up high because I don't want to fall off a chair and break a hip.

Instead I've put them in the lowest cupboard as far back as I could get them so any visiting adult children looking for a sugar fix don't swipe them. I stop and ask myself how badly I want this comfort food. I've made it a month without any.

In a heartbeat, my entire upper body is swallowed by the cupboard blocking all light so I'm searching by feel alone. My hand finds the Halloween cookie cutters I haven't used in fifteen years but hold on to like an old favorite bra.

Bingo! I wiggle and back my way out of the cupboard bumping my head only twice and flip myself around into a sitting position on the floor. Remembering the good posture my Yaya drilled into me, I lean against a closed cupboard.

With my robe askew I'm rather unladylike with my legs out straight and open like a happy child. One Scooby pointed to the ceiling and the other upside down on the floor, I smile to no one but myself and tear the bag open.

The rule is I take out one and put the bag back so I'll think twice before I have another.

This time I don't want to be my own mother. I make a decision, take the entire bag of chocolate to my bedroom and flip on the light to read a book. Next thing I know, the sun is up, the book is on my chest, there's melted chocolate on my cheek and I have a sugar hangover. I should have listened to the mother me.

* * *

The drawback to contacts other than never being able to own a convertible, is rubbing an eye. How could I forget this no-no? A lens can stay in the same exact spot for months as long as I do not rub my eye even slightly when it's closed.

The minute I touch my closed eyelid and open my eye, the world is a hazy mess on one side. I freeze and carefully look around for the lost lens. After I blink once or twice, I know exactly where it is.

The sensation of having a contact lens stuck under my eyelid feels like someone wadded up the aluminum foil covering a 27 pound turkey and jammed it between my eyeball and eyelid.

How can anything that feels so huge, be so hard to find?

I blink hoping it will come down. I hold my eye closed while I look up hoping to "catch" the lens and I've tried closing the eye and rubbing the contact down to where it belongs.

When this fails, and it usually does, the next step is the eye flush. A quart of saline solution sometimes works. On occasion I find the offending contact in the pool of saline on the table I was leaning over to do the flush.

By then, whether it works or not, it still feels like the contact is crammed under my eyelid. I get frustrated and rub my eye to ease the itch and burn and when I next see my face in the mirror, my eye is so red and swollen it looks like I just got up from a knock out round in the ring.

I don't care. It's not like I'm going to reapply any makeup because it won't help a darn thing.

One time I was convinced the contact had fallen out and I just didn't see it. I popped in another one and went about my business. A month later my vision wasn't right. I took out the contact to clean it and found two.

Glasses and Contacts

I tried wearing bifocal contacts. It made me dizzier than spinning circles in my underwear.

Using contacts for distance and reading glasses for close up means that there is an area that won't focus in the middle, right at about three to four feet. It made me look like a chicken bobbing back and forth trying to get things in focus.

Once the chicken exercise got rid of the double chin that was forming I partially fixed the problem by wearing two or three pair of glasses.

Being that I put the ch in cheap, I buy my reading glasses at the dollar store and they double as a hair accessory. I avoid the granny spectacle chains by wearing my glasses atop my head.

Keeps my hair out of my face and I can wear up to three pair up there at the same time. Only twice in the past five years has someone come up and pointed out I had extra glasses on my head.

Since each pair amplifies the last, I am now proud to say I can once again thread a needle.

Other times I get so frustrated, I just pretend I can see. I mean as long as I have a general idea of what I'm looking at, it's not as bad as my father pretending he could hear us kids and then answer a question we didn't ask, is it?

6

The Nose - Why Don't Boobs Keep Growing Instead?

I think we should get to choose which part of our body continues to grow. I mean why does it have to be the nose? You can be born with an adorable button nose and end up with a beak.

Or like my father, you can have a handsome nose that later grows a hook at the end.

If I could choose, I'd probably pick my legs over my nose, although a growing bosom might have saved me a few dollars.

One of my exes always said I needed shin implants (I swore I simply had long thighs). Still, if my legs grew I wouldn't have stayed at a whopping five foot tall since I was eleven-years-old and I would be able to eat more being taller, or, at least *look* thinner!

Anyway, I like my nose and always have. I guess I have this fear after years of my father teasing me. When I was little, he'd put me on his knee and inspect my nose. Then he would say, "Ah, I see it. The beginning of the hook! You are going to have a nose just like me!"

I would run panic stricken to the mirror and check my face. While my nose is smaller, I swear at 57 I can see that hook beginning to form. Heck, I'm probably manifesting it right now.

Nose Hair

The last place I expected to see hair was protruding from my nostrils. I had never seen nose hair on a woman in my life. The meanest part of it all is that I couldn't see it when it happened. Lucky for me, my kids were and still are always willing to point out my imperfections.

Here's a bit of conversation from the past...

"Uh Mom, are you going to do anything about that nose hair?"

"What nose hair?" I asked since I was sure my son was kidding.

"Seriously Mother, you should do something about that."

I ran to the mirror. Apparently the light was bad because I couldn't see it and I was only 45 years old at the time.

I saw my son standing behind my reflection. Surely my 14-year-old was pranking me.

"You see it?"

"I don't have hair hanging out of my nose, and that's not funny."

"Get your glasses Ma."

Oh my God! He was right! How could I have prided myself on my femininity when who knows how long I'd been parading this face with perfect makeup all over town with ...*n o s e   h a i r*

"Quick," I barked, "Where's the tiny scissors?"

Before he could answer, my arms flailed as I tore apart the bathroom drawer so I could fix this behemoth problem.

Poking myself a half dozen times, I snipped and snipped. Then I made all three of my kids do a nose hair check. I had solved the problem.

A week later, they were back.

I kept the tiny scissors and a pair of reading glasses in my makeup bag so I could snip every few days. It got old and I was always afraid someone at work might catch a glimpse of the real ape woman.

One brave day I made an undercover trip to the pharmacy and pretended I was buying a nose hair shaver for the husband I didn't have. Surely this would be the answer to my nose's beastly appearance.

Carefully I used it. It tickled and pulled; hurt and shocked; but it worked for a few months. The day it gave me a good shock *and* made my nose bleed from an interior cut, I threw the thing out.

What do I do now?

Pluck.

Yes ma'am, I do. It makes eyebrow plucking a walk in the park with an ice cream cone.

And, I can attest to the fact it makes the eyes water as much as sniffing a gallon jug of ammonia or cutting a dozen raw onions.

Since it gets the job done and lasts awhile I do it. I try to do it right after I get out of the shower thinking the pores are more open then so they come out easier. Besides, if my eyes are watering when I leave the bathroom, it looks like it's from my shower.

Pimples and Pores

I had a week between my pimples leaving and my wrinkles showing up. I had thought a few decades would be fairer, but what do I know?

My major nose zit problem was with blackheads. They weren't as noticeable as a whopper on the cheek but close inspection drove me to pick and squeeze at them until they *looked* like the whoppers on my cheek.

Well the blackheads are long gone and there are no wrinkles on my nose but I've still got a gripe. When did the pores on my nose start looking like empty volcanic craters? How can a hole grow? I'm starting to miss my blackheads.

7

I Missed Tongue Day at Insecurity School

If you haven't critiqued your tongue, you are probably too well adjusted and have self esteem.

Let me help you get the ball rolling on this one so you know whether you have a normal tongue; an oversized monster or an embarrassment that should never be let out in public.

We start out thinking we are normal. It's not until we go to insecurity school do we learn to compare all our features with everyone else. And the tongue is a difficult feature to compare because it's pretty much hidden away for its entire life.

I missed tongue day at insecurity school so I thought mine was just fine. In my twenties, when I needed to see the dentist on a regular basis, I began to wonder.

I loved the guy and it didn't hurt that he was nice looking. After over a dozen visits in the chair, he finally said something that would change my life forever.

"Andrea, can you please hold your tongue still? It's hard to work in your mouth when your tongue keeps following my fingers. I'm beginning to feel molested in here."

My face turned beet red. I was mortified. To the best of my Novocain ability, I said, "Ut how cun I contro it en it iz num?"

"Just try. I'm afraid I'm going to get it with the drill."

Later, I did an at-home inspection. It looked okay but I'd seen it for years. How was I to know? By then I was on husband number two so I asked him to show me his tongue.

Oh my god! I was shocked. It was a short skinny thing that reminded me of a bird's tongue. No wonder he was a lousy kisser. Compared to his, mine looked like a beaver tail.

To top it off, he could roll his making it look more like a straw.

Now what's with that? How is it that some folks can roll their tongue like a carpet while the rest of ours just lie there? And others can roll a tongue the other way so it looks like a mini bowl.

I felt deprived. No matter how hard I tried to do these oral gymnastics, I couldn't do them. I was stuck with a untalented fleshy organ, its only claim to fame was tasting everything in its path.

And taste it does. Constantly exploring the confines of its cave, even my teeth get tired of being molested because about once a week, when my tongue gets too personal, they bite it.

8

Who Stole My Lips?

While I was busy bemoaning the growing wrinkles on my forehead and around my eyes, my lips were headed for the exit.

My once full lips started with a tricky fade so I wouldn't notice what was coming next. The fade seemed a small price to pay in the aging process. I smiled and took it like a woman.

The truth hit me one afternoon while putting on lipstick to give them a color boost.

I ran the lipstick across my upper lip first and noticed I'd gone out of bounds. Once I corrected it, I wanted to cry.

Where did they go? My lower lip was smaller but I couldn't stop staring at my upper sliver lip. I had to admit to myself I was truly falling apart.

I tried different facial expressions in the mirror to make my upper lip visible to the naked eye. This only increased the above-lip wrinkles. Closer inspection (meaning two pair of reading glasses) revealed the ugly truth. It resembled a raisin having a bad day and needing to be replumped with a warm water bath.

It was like walking by the goldfish bowl and realizing your kid's fish is swimming in half the water it had last time you looked. While I'd been busy making sure the dogs, cats, chickens, ferrets had been fed and cleaned up after; the poor quiet goldfish had been overlooked. And now my lips had evaporated as well.

I used to look like I was always pouting because my bottom lip was a bit bigger than my top. What was I complaining about? At least I HAVE a bottom lip. My top lip seems to have disappeared and if I were a man I'd grow a mustache to cover it up.

Wait! I'm half Greek, if I stop shaving, plucking or waxing I'll have a mustache to cover up my upper lip in nine days… but I don't think it'll go with my boobs, which by the grace of god, are still standing… pretty much. (Okay, at least they don't disappear into my armpits when I lie on my back.)

Those Wrinkles Above the Lip

While doing lip exercises in front of the mirror, I found a cure for those sneaky little wrinkles at the upper lip's edge. There are some side effects but who cares. What's the cure?

Smiling! Yes, not only does smiling make them spread out and disappear, the side effects are purely tolerable. There's a better frame of mind and improved disposition. This creates happiness and makes it much easier to laugh.

I just have to remember to stop smiling when someone is telling me a sad story or why their day has gone to hell in a hand basket. It could ruin a relationship.

Once the lip wrinkle problem was handled without a facelift, I had time to get back to the size and fading dilemma. I'm thinking about getting a little color tattooed. After all, if my neighbor could get eyebrows tattooed on her face, why shouldn't I have lips? I'd try collagen but I'm afraid it would go south like everything else and my double chin would come back.

Stupid Habits

One of the reasons I have those above lip wrinkles is that I smoke cigarettes. Of course it's stupid but if I were perfect what would I have to write about?

I tried to smoke cigarettes without puckering up but I was sucking air. I thought about quitting but I already had the wrinkles so what was the point.

Smoking cigarettes was a choice and I had good reason to start smoking when I was twelve. I had been a thumb sucker since before birth. My mother had tried everything to get me to stop which ultimately made it worse. Here were a few tactics.

- "Take that thumb out of your mouth!" (I heard this 27 times a day in my third and fourth year of life.)

- "You can't go to kindergarten as a thumb sucker. The other kids will make fun of you." (This method was applied 14 times a day during my fourth and fifth year. I hid under my blanket at school nap time.)

- "You're going to get buck teeth." (I practiced with

care not to push against my teeth with my thumb and never got buck teeth.)

- She once made me wear gloves for a week. Thumb sucking wasn't something I thought about. It was automatic. Getting a furry fibrous thumb was uncomfortable, so I'd retreat to my room, take the thumb out of the glove and proceed as normal.

- Pepper on the thumb didn't last either

By the ripe old age of seven, I only put my thumb in my mouth during sleep. I would sleep with my head completely under the covers so no one would know but Mom figured it out.

Finally when I was twelve, Mama made a comment that scared the pants off me.

"No one will ever marry you if you suck your thumb."

This put the fear of God in me since I wanted to be a wife and mother more than just about anything.

The plan was, I would smoke on occasion when I had the urge to suck my thumb. This would cure me of problem number one. Quitting cigarettes would be a piece of cake after quitting the thumb.

This was the first of a long line of foolish mistakes.

I met Husband #1 when I was fourteen. He didn't care in the least that I had a thumb addiction. At nineteen we married and smoked cigarettes together during waking hours and I comforted myself with thumb sucking at night without shame.

I happily released endorphins at night until the age of forty one and the removal of a tumor in my face.

Try as I might, I could not leave my thumb in my

mouth. The nerve damage in my face left me with almost no feeling or control at all on one side. Not only could I not tell if my thumb was in there, I didn't want to bite it off while sleeping. It took six months to learn how to sleep without my faithful companion.

Eventually most of my facial nerves grew back but the habit was gone. I miss my thumb.

9

Teeth Improve Your Smile

Ever play out little scenarios in your head? The way you'd like it to go or something you wish you had the nerve to do or say? Most of mine were with my husbands and how each one realized I was the most wonderful woman in the world and they were fools to ever think otherwise. (Obviously, it didn't happen or I wouldn't have had three husbands.)

Here's my favorite: I tell him *exactly* what's wrong with him, and it feels great to get it off my chest. Instead of him trying to run me over with his truck, he has an epiphany about how he's done me wrong; he changes right then and there, and life goes on like an old Nelson Eddy/Jeanette McDonald or Fred Astaire/Ginger Rogers movie (without the dancing, since I've never been smart enough to marry a man who could or would dance) and we happily grow old together and die in our sleep.

Of course if I told you one of those scenarios, inevitably I would get sued. After all I'm sure they all think they are perfect and wouldn't take kindly to my revealing anything about our past relationships.

The subject of this chapter being *Teeth*, here's a little scenario about them.

I'm with a group of young adults at my kid's 25th birthday. With mixed drinks in our hands and snacking on hors d'oeuvres, someone says, "You've got something between your teeth."

I say, "Really?" and just pop out the top denture. I proceed to use the bottom tip of my blouse, pick it out and buff off my dentures and pop them back in with a smile and the comment, "Thanks, got it!"

Of course this scenario is ridiculous because at my kid's birthday bash there would be beer and chips. No pate, crab or artichoke dip and certainly no high priced alcohol unless you could count a bottle of Jack Daniels being passed around for everyone to take a swig.

Me and my daydreaming!

...Now you know I have dentures. It sucks, so, I'm going to tell you all about them. If you don't have them, thank your lucky stars. If you do and they fit, thank your lucky stars.

* * *

As a warm up before I talk teeth, let's start with gums. Why do gums recede?

Seeing others with badly receding gums reminds me of a horse. Horses are utterly gorgeous creatures, yet when they open their mouths enough to see all their teeth, it's enough to scare the pants off you.

...One day after brushing my teeth and giving the mirror a big grin, I was stopped dead in my tracks. Good lord, the tooth fairy must have snuck into my room in the middle of the night and pushed them back with my cuticle pusher.

Was business slow that night?

It's true I'd focused a great deal on my teeth. Convinced my parents had dentures because they'd grown up in the Great Depression and gone without dental care, I was going to do everything to be sure I kept mine.

The thought of putting my teeth in a glass at night just grossed me out to no end.

I'd brushed, flossed and water picked my way to perfect oral hygiene and had all my dental checkups.

I did whatever the dentists told me to do, to no avail. I had lots of fillings. I had at least eight root canals. I had several crowns.

I was told the reason I couldn't chew an ice cube, let ice cream touch my teeth and got cavities easily was because of thin enamel.

Even after insurance, I had thousands and thousands of dollars invested in my mouth so I could keep my teeth beautiful my entire life.

If I had spent my dental money on a good wardrobe instead maybe I could have married into a family with money enough to take care of my teeth.

The funniest part was I thought all the work I had done was permanent! Okay, so it wasn't funny. Imagine my surprise when once I lost my dental insurance, in my mid forties, my crowns started falling off.

Maybe quitting my job and going into business with my third husband wasn't the smartest move on the planet. Determination and working 15 to 18 hours a day didn't make us rich.

In fact we lost the business and I continued losing teeth.

As a 57th birthday present, the free clinic pulled my

remaining twenty teeth and gave me Tylenol for the pain. (I haven't always been a famous author. I think it's been about a week now.)

How did I handle my predicament? I hid at home, emailed a lot... and I practiced.

I practiced never letting my lips go in. The "sunk in" look grosses me out. I practiced smiling without opening my mouth and lord have mercy I had to learn to speak all over again.

Ever tried to make the *'th'* sound without teeth? Sounds like a snake hissing, but I had my dignity to uphold.

I talked to myself. I talked to the dogs, the birds and the plants outside. I spoke slowly when I answered the phone ...and I got it!

After putting every possible combination of food through the blender and losing 40 pounds, it seemed I was going to have to get some teeth. Besides, I had a huge event coming up that rain, sleet or snow couldn't keep me from.

My eldest son was getting married and I was tired of those little scenarios playing out in my head where I'm at the wedding and show all 300 guests a huge and utterly toothless grin.

And I forgot to mention, trusting people can occasionally go wrong. The second part of my birthday present was coming home to find a bank representative posting a notice that we had 30 days to vacate the premises. Someone had not been making the house payments.

I sold all but a few of my worldly possessions between Craigslist and garage sales. I left my beloved Georgia when my youngest son flew in, rescued me and the dog, towing my little trailer of worldly possessions to his home

1200 miles north.

Getting Dentures

The only time I use the word dentures, is in this book. Dentures are for old people and I won't be old for another 30 or 40 years. Therefore, I got teeth.

After countless impressions and testing, the day arrived for me to go pick up my new teeth. Talk about excited! I wondered if the dentist would just hand them to me in a gift bag or have me try them on first.

"They have to be fitted." he said.

"Well, what were all those fittings for already? You made impressions and the lab made wax molds for my gums. The lab put teeth in them and adjusted them three times and now they're supposed to be perfect.

"Not quite," he laughed as he put them in for me and brought out a little piece of carbon paper.

"Chomp, chomp, chomp and grind," he said in his nicest voice. Then he took them out and started grinding.

This process was repeated for 30 minutes.

"Okay" he said, "Now you can wear them for two hours today and four hours tomorrow. You will have sore spots. Let them get red and irritated so I can see where I need to adjust next time, but don't let them get infected.

Get infected? Holy shit, my heart sank and he may have caught me doing an eye roll. Still, I had teeth and I was grateful. I walked out smiling. Surely I wouldn't have to go back right?

Are Dentures Frustrating? Of Course Not!

It felt like I had a boot in my mouth, but I'm guessing the taste was more like a Crock sandal.

It hurt to close my lips and somehow they felt more like those plastic Dracula teeth I wore as a kid on Halloween. I checked the rear view mirror. They didn't look like Dracula teeth. They looked darned real.

I decided to practice my smile, and practice I did. I beamed the entire ten miles home.

By the time I got there, my upper lip was stuck to my teeth, so I pried it off. Apparently the bulk of my saliva was floating around under my dentures because it felt like they were floating as well.

My daughter came by shortly after I got home and we talked outside for twenty minutes before she squealed, "Mom! You got teeth!"

Was the girl blind? I looked like Harry the Horse (but I must admit the huge contraption in my mouth stretched and made my mouth wrinkles practically disappear.)

And there was one other thing my girl didn't notice. I sounded funny when I talked! Once again I would have to go back to the mirror; learn to smile and speak in a whole new way. Why is life always about changing?

While I was thinking about all I had to do in the next three weeks before the upcoming nuptials so that I didn't embarrass my son, his bride or myself, my daughter spoke.

"Oh God Mom, they're beautiful! I love them!"

"Thanks," I beamed.

"And they look better than mine."

"Plus I don't have to floss," I smiled.

"Oh Mom you're so funny. Can I see them?"

"You want me to take them out???"

"YES! Come on ...Uncle Jammie never took out his fake eye for me so the least you can do is let me hold your teeth."

"You're weird but I love you. Okay, I'll take them out

but let's go inside."

I popped out my pearly whites, rinsed them off in the kitchen sink; patted them dry and handed them to her.

"Cool!" (Spoken like a true 19-year-old.) "Oh my God Mom, they have your name on them!"

"Well, that's in case I get into a bar room brawl with another old lady and our teeth fly out. It would be much easier to tell whose teeth are whose, when it's all over."

"Oh Mom!"

"Or maybe it was so they didn't get them mixed up with someone else's at the teeth factory."

"That makes sense. What have you eaten?"

"Nothing yet."

"Well, put them in and eat! I'll watch."

I was having one of those moments where I wasn't so sure it was a good idea that I raised my kids to be open with me about everything.

My son had left some raw almonds on the counter that had been making me drool for days. I love almonds. I thought I'd pop one in and munch down but with the first attempt, I hit the front of my teeth with the almond.

Apparently those teeth were taking up a lot more room than their predecessors.

Why is it that I thought I was just getting teeth instead of teeth WITH GUMS? If you've ever seen a snake eat its prey, you'll know how I felt. I had to disengage my jaw to open my mouth wide enough to get food in there. And it was just an almond!

I quickly learned that by chewing on one side, the other side of the denture would pop up, allowing food fragments to sneak underneath. I then tried one almond on each side at the same time. It made my gums hurt.

This was going to take a lot of work, plus I was going to have to go get that teeth glue goo. Needless to say, I didn't make the whole two hours the dentist advised. Nuts are probably not a good first food because after 3 of them I was ready to retire my chompers, and have a good cry.

* * *

Back to the dentist I went for more chomp, grind, chomp; but things weren't feeling much better.

The following weekend my eldest son and his fiancé invited me to play putt-putt. He had yet to see my teeth.

As we walked into the indoor pee wee golf course ...in front of God and everyone he stood facing me and said, "Let me see your teeth."

I gave him a huge grin to give him a good look.

"Hmm," he said, "How do they work? Let me see the gum part."

I pulled my upper lip out like an orangutan and he tilted his head peering into my mouth. Somehow I began feeling rather self conscious (I'm very sensitive) and I decided it was time to do something about it.

"Would you like me to just pop them out and hand them to you?"

That did it. "No, no, no. Sorry, I was just so curious. Let's play."

Good choice son.

Mini golf was a blast. I love my kids and I love doing things with them. Afterward, they treated me to pizza. They thought it would be easy for me to eat and so did I.

What I learned was this:

A large bite of pizza crust once wet, acts like glue. It adheres not only to your dentures, but to the new plastic roof of your mouth. My tongue couldn't budge the stuff.

I kept working at it but it felt like the pizza crust glued

my teeth together as well. When prying the mouth back open, something has to give and that would be the lower dentures.

As my lower teeth rattled around in my mouth, I excused myself and went to the ladies room for washing and re-gluing. After that, I ate tiny little pieces of pizza and finished my first slice about 20 minutes after they were done with the rest of the pizza. My mouth was in pain.

Back to the dentist I went for more chomp, grind, chomp.

This same son wanting to see me happy and joyous invited me over for one of my favorite meals. Steak! Something I hadn't had in ages.

Usually he grills them to perfection so they are good and pink inside, tender and easy to chew.

Oops!

Actually there were two oops. The first was I lost track of time. In a hurry, I headed out the door late to go to his house. I stopped for gas and got half way to his house (a 30 minute drive) when I realized I'd left something important at home.

Cursing, I pulled an almost legal U-turn. En route, my daughter called my cell. She was coming for dinner too and wanted a ride.

"No problem," I said. "Meet me at the house in five minutes."

She pulled in as I was locking the front door behind me. She jumped in the car and we headed out. "Mom, I'm confused. Tyler said you left the house 40 minutes ago."

"I did Boo, but I forgot something and had to come back."

"What was so important for you to drive all the way back?"

"My teeth!"

"How could you forget your teeth?"

"I don't like the damn things. They hurt! I only put them in when I leave the house. Now don't tell your brother."

We arrived late. My son graciously handed me a beer. We talked a few minutes and then he said, "Mom, you called to let me know you were leaving the house over an hour ago. What happened to you?"

"I forgot my teeth." I'm pretty sure it was my honesty that made his beer go down the wrong pipe and gave him a coughing fit.

Good thing my daughter didn't tattle on me.

When dinner was served, I was excited. I was also the center of attention. "Mom, I'm so sorry, I overcooked the steaks. Is yours okay? Can you eat it?"

"Of course I can eat it honey. It's great." Okay, so maybe I was lying through my new teeth. It tasted wonderful but chewing wasn't going very well. After the first bite my mouth hurt ...a lot.

What could I do? I love my kid and I love steak. It was a big deal that he would do this for me and I was not going to cry in front of him. Plus he was watching me. What did I do?

I cut it in tiny pieces, pretended I was chewing and swallowed the pieces whole. An hour later I took his dog outside to throw the ball. I didn't want anyone to hear the noises coming from my stomach ...or the sound effects I knew would follow.

* * *

I was getting tired of going to the dentist. After another two trips for chomp, chomp, grind and file, I'd about had it. I don't think my discount dentist liked me so much anymore either. I was frustrated and he was talking about charging me extra. It wasn't my fault.

I'd watched and watched how he did the adjustments and I was down to one week before the wedding. I still hadn't managed to eat a whole meal.

Bright and early a few days later (meaning noon), my youngest son woke and followed the sound of a power tool into the kitchen.

"Sorry to wake you so early," I said poised over the kitchen sink.

"What the hell are you doing?"

"Fixing my damn teeth," I smiled politely with my lips closed.

"Ma what if you ruin them?"

"Well Darlin', I can't make them any worse. The wedding is next week and I can't even keep them in 2 hours. On the big day I've got to keep them in at least nine hours plus I have to eat in front of 300 people.

What may be even worse is the rehearsal dinner the night before. This will be the first time I've seen your father and his wife in five years. I'd rather my teeth don't fall out on my plate and make her day.

Here are the facts:

1. I can't close my mouth comfortably. If I smoke a cigarette or kiss someone it makes the inside of my mouth bleed.

2. I've watched the dentist mark and grind them so many times, I understand the procedure.

3. Lucky for me, I've got 102 bits and grinding stones for my Dremel tool. Surely that's enough to do the job."

"Oh my God Ma".
"It'll work out honey."
"And what if it doesn't?"
"I'll smile a lot, feign lack of hunger and hope I don't get drunk and pass out on my plate since I'm not a heavyweight when it comes to alcohol."

He walked away shaking his head but my efforts paid off.

* * *

After a year of anticipation, I was dressed and on my way to the wedding rehearsal. For as little food as I ate, I should have weighed 20 pounds less but my body was in 'concentration camp' modality, allowing me to maintain my plump weight on a mere 1500 calories a day.

Lucky me!

Assuming there would be a truce between my ex husband's wife and I, I concentrated on holding in my stomach so I looked better. In hindsight, I should have concentrated more on walking in my high heels. Since I was out of practice, my ankle gave way walking across the lawn at the hotel right in front of her.

I never understood why she hated me. I certainly didn't hate her. All I had to do was sit near her during the rehearsal ceremony. To make things easier afterward, my son had me sit with him and his betrothed, instead of at the parents of the bride and groom table. That was fine by me.

As it turned out, my kid's step-mom was a trouper.

Not only was she kind and considerate, she invited me to sit next to *her* at the dinner. With six of us at the table (5 parents and my youngest son who sat on the other side of me for support) the conversation was enjoyable.

While I had a bit of trouble eating my calamari appetizer, I was in luck that salmon and a lovely soft potato dish were on the menu. I ordered it.

The groom stared at me from across our private room at the restaurant. When I excused myself to use the restroom to re-glue my pearly whites, he followed me out into the hall.

"Are you okay?! I'm so sorry. You weren't supposed to sit next to her. You were supposed to sit with us."

"Honey, don't look a gift horse in the mouth," I said with floating lowers. "She invited me. Either she doesn't hate me anymore or she's making a good show for everyone. It doesn't matter. It's working and I'm enjoying myself."

I gave him a hug and my daughter followed me to the restroom while I pried the food out of the underside of my lowers, rinsed them and sprinkled a good dose of powdered adhesive to keep my teeth from disengaging again. Gluing my lips together was just an accident.

* * *

The wedding was beautiful. My ex and his wife bought me a few drinks in the bar before the ceremony and dang, if that woman didn't put her arm around me during the ceremony when I cried. That was our boy up there.

More Fun with Dentures

It's possible that in the past several months of having

dentures, I've had more bad experiences with them than husbands. That's hard to say for sure since I tend to focus on the present.

Here are a few fun discoveries:

- Receding gums are a thing of the past since I got new gums with my teeth.
- Not enough Polygrip makes my lowers come loose with the first bite of food. If food gets under there and I keep chewing, my gums bleed.

- Too much Polygrip tends to ooze out the sides giving my food the additional flavor of minty toothpaste. Yumbo!
- Also, being overzealous with the goo, glues unsuspecting parts.... I have glued my lips together several times.

Getting them apart is no problem but wiping off the adhesive leaves my fingers sticky; or the feeling of paper towel fragments left behind.

- I'm thinking about trying it on some deep wrinkles to fill them in or glue them closed.
- Dentures protect the mouth from below freezing temperatures. I breathe through my mouth when jogging. The other day the dog and I did a short run and I realized breathing didn't hurt even when my hands were numb.
- My restless tongue keeps trying to play peek-a-boo by pulling up my dentures in search of my real teeth.

- It is entirely possible for a long head hair to work its way under my lower teeth on a windy day while still attached to my head!

And most important of all, I can smile all I want and the more I smile, the more I want to!

10

When Cleaning and Ironing Don't Work

I expected the holes for my pierced earrings to turn to slits, but one of them is hidden in a giant wrinkle. If starch would work, I'd spray it on and iron my earlobe.

I didn't think anyone under the age of 90 had wrinkled ears but maybe I just didn't notice. Like the tongue thing. I'm going to have to do a quick study while in line at the grocery store on senior citizens day. The tabloids are hardly worth reading anymore since I don't even know this generation of movie stars or other famous folks.

They all look like teeny boppers to me and personally, I think they're just a bunch of whiners. The gain or loss of 20 pounds is peanuts compared to what they're going to experience in another twenty or thirty years and boy are they going to love their tattoos after a few decades...if they can remember what they used to be.

And divorce? Been there done that. They should shut

up and appreciate their multimillion dollar divorce settlements. Shit, I would have been happy with a running car.

Huh? What? Say That Again?

Since I've heard people are like their dogs, I was hoping hair had grown in my ears. Not because I want hairy ears but it seemed the Greek thing to do. Besides, I pluck or shave everything else, so what the heck. If I did and it improved my hearing I'd be thrilled.

The kids get mad I ask the word "What?" on a regular basis. They think I am hard of hearing. I think they slur their words. What I am is short on a frequency or two. If Daddy were here, I'd apologize to him for not understanding what he went through. Now I understand why some senior citizens turn off their hearing aids.

I notice when watching a movie, music and sound effects are too loud and the dialogue is too quiet.

Listening to my kids on the phone is frustration at its finest. It sounds like they're yelling too near the microphone because they sound loud and garbled. For example, if I say…"What?", they will speak louder, making it even worse. Apparently they don't know the meaning of enunciate.

On the sneaky side, I can hear whispers loud and clear. I won't admit to what I've heard because I know one of my kids will read this book and spill the beans. As to what I heard my spouse say doesn't matter either. I'll just say we now live in different states.

11

Wasn't it Suppose to be One Chin Per Neck?

I want to coin a new phrase right now. Chinneck!

I was blessed with a chin and had a second one for awhile but two was not better than one. It sort of ruined the definition between the chin and the neck.

I used to think that wattle joke was really funny... until my dog Helen pinched the shit out of me one night licking my neck and the extra skin must have caught somewhere because it ended up between her teeth. It hurt!

I squealed like a girl and ran to the mirror to check for a wattle. Apparently I'm pre-wattle. But it still left a mark like a great big hickey.

That means my neck skin has lost elasticity but nothing is sagging to date.

Why did I have to bring this up? I now find myself compelled to do the Jack La Lanne neck exercise as I write this chapter. Thank God I joined my mom at 7am back in the 60s. We'd exercise with him in front of our black and white television.

All of us were there...me, Mom, Jack, his wife Elaine and his white German Shepherd named Max.

Jack was my very first exercise instructor and will always have a special place in my heart. It might even have something to do with him that I own a Champion Juicer and adore fresh carrot juice.

While I know I giggled when I was five or six, I'm no longer laughing at the neck exercise.

Come on, do it with me now. But never do this in public unless you're trying to scare off a mugger or trying to make friends with an orangutan.

It's best not to do it in front of the mirror either. Heck, even Jack and his wife Elaine looked silly doing this.

With head upright, make your bottom jaw come out and up. Your bottom teeth should make your upper lip nearly disappear. Repeat 20 times. Tilt your head back to stretch out those neck muscles. Hold to the count of ten. Now do it again.

Didn't think you could get a sore neck this way did ya? But doesn't it feel thinner already? This is great if you want to get back down to one chin also.

I do have a warning. If you do *not* do this exercise and your extra chin or waddle disappear, check under your arms.

Remember how Popeye's muscle used to look when he flexed and hadn't had his spinach? You know I'm talking about those little flaps that start out the size of wings on feminine pads and grow from there.

I hate those things. If my arms are going to have wings, they should be big enough to fly with, not just flap around making slapping noises and looking ridiculous.

12

Boobs, the Fraternal Twins

Breasts are a wonderful thing.

What are breasts for? To feed babies! Of course they double as a sexual object receiving wonderful attention our entire lives. Amen.

Men and women alike are obsessed with breasts. Men want to see them, talk about them and give them undying devotion while women want men to talk about them, look at them and give them undying devotion.

Bras

We are shallow when it comes to our breasts. Stupid ego! Even after their prime, we stuff them into bras that push, shove and manipulate them to look their best. Some of us flaunt them and others keep them covered, but underneath, when the girls look good in a bra, we stand taller, walk straighter and feel pretty.

I'm glad that at my age I know how to wear a bra. I'm

talking about the fit, not which way it goes on. I don't know who invented the darn things but I thought they were supposed to support the twins to keep gravity at bay.

Back in the day, when you went to buy a bra, you got fitted. I miss that. None of these young gals know how to wear a bra properly. The back strap is not supposed to be at the neckline for God's sake.

I still remember what my mom and the lady at Sears taught me.

The bra is supposed to go straight around, level with the bottom of the bosoms. That's what they used to call them. Isn't that a respectable name?)

Adjust the hooks in the back so sits firmly around you without slipping or sliding; but not too tight as to make breathing difficult or make you look like you have fat bulging out.

Adjust the straps so they don't fall off your shoulders but not so high that they raise the back of the brazier above the bottom of your boob line. Then do the final check:

- Raise your hands over your head
- Bend over and touch your toes

If everything stays where it was, and you can still breathe, you have a winner. If your boobs popped out when you bent over; if the bra raised up on top of your boobs when you lifted your hands/arms above your head... I don't care how pretty or sexy the bra is... put it back!

* * *

The first words I heard for the twins were bosoms and breasts. I think that's womanly and natural reminding me of works by Michelangelo. See what I mean?

Yet they have a myriad of names, some are rather descriptive and some are just, well, rude. Eventually I loosened up and stopped being bothered by their titles.

I've come a long way baby (remember that commercial?)

Here is a sampling. These are the ones I find acceptable, don't find especially offensive or laugh out loud when I hear them. But maybe I haven't come as far as I thought ...the list holds 125 names.

Bosoms, breasts, boobs, boobies, tits, titties, tatas, a rack, the twins, the girls, knockers, hooters, headlights, jugs, melons, cantaloupes, tomatoes, puppies, gazongas, bazoombas, flapjacks and pancakes.

Some of these you'll notice are rather descriptive for different phases of the life of our boobs. Let's face it, they go through more changes than any other body part. It matters not that the whole world can't see them. We have eyes.

Heck I don't think I got over the fact my twins were fraternal and not identical until I was 45. Silly woman!

The life of our boobs can be summed up by an old Frank Sinatra song called "That's Life"

I've been up, and down, and over and out; and I know one thing. Each time I find myself flat on my face I pick myself up and get back in the race. That's life! (Now is that a bra story or what?)

Another part of the same song makes me laugh because it describes breasts by their seasons in life and lead to a story...

Your riding high in April, shot down in May. But I know I'm gonna change that tune when I'm back on top, back on top in June. I said that's life!

My Own Girls (Serious Stuff)

We're up to the true confessions part of the book. Why not? If I tell the dirt on me, no one else can do it. There will be no surprises to embarrass me later. Instead I can be embarrassed now and get it over with.

It's not like there are any naked pictures of me floating around on the internet, and besides, at my age, who would want to see them anyway? That's not quite the kind of dirt I'm talking about.

(But bless you for having a dirty mind. Some good things we should never lose.)

* * *

Puberty came and left. I'd had high hopes of looking like Rachel Welch instead of my mother. Obviously I didn't understand genetics.

Falling for the ridiculous notion that in order to be feminine or sexy I needed to be a size C or D cup with substantial cleavage, I grew up feeling a lack of fulfillment and femininity.

Never mind that I had a tiny waist and a substantial booty. I did everything I could to improve the twins appearance, but you can't do a whole lot with fried eggs, sunny side up.

Being set apart, the twins didn't have cleavage even when shoved around so I tried eye shadow. Someone asked if I spilled something.

Perky but no bulge, I tried wearing push up bras. On a

date, I bent over to pick up a dropped earring on the dance floor and they both popped out.

Things were not going well when trying to look breastful.

In my mid 20's I gave up.

"I am what I am" I would say to myself, "And I should be grateful they're still standing."

At 31, I became pregnant with my first child. I was excited.

In my fourth month I asked my OBGYN when I was going to get boobs. He laughed.

"What's so funny? I thought all women's boobs got bigger with pregnancy. Are you telling me I am NOT going to look like Rachel Welch or Gina Lollobrigida even for awhile?"

"Not all women do."

"Great, lost out again. Maybe I'll get implants after I'm done having children."

He ignored me and went back to talking about the baby.

* * *

After my son was born, I got my first glimpse of having real breasts. It hurt. They weren't huge but they were certainly fuller and I remember being angry at the pediatrician who took one look at me and told me I would have to supplement my son's feeding with formula.

It was one thing to not have big gorgeous breasts like a famous actress. That's just wish list stuff. But to have the audacity to tell me they were too puny to do their god given job just fried my butt.

To prove that man wrong I nursed my son whenever he seemed to need it. Perhaps I was a bit overzealous. He fed every two hours round the clock and at four months old, weighed in at 20 pounds.

"He's a big boy," exclaimed the pediatrician. "What kind of cereal are you feeding?"

"None! I'm just breastfeeding."

He looked from my son to my chest. I swear he nearly giggled. It was obvious he thought I was lying.

I changed the subject. "Doctor," I said, "I'm worried that he hasn't rolled over yet. He seems perfectly healthy and happy but shouldn't he be turning over by now?"

"I think you need to put it in perspective. He's like a little sumo wrestler. He's got a lot more to turn over than most babies. I mean how would you turn over if you weighed 300 pounds?"

Shortly after that I got a new pediatrician.

About the time milk production went down, the girls began looking a little sad. Every time I got out of the shower and saw myself in the mirror, all I could think of was Aspen because I sure wasn't looking at Heavenly Valley. Things were not looking good.

At 38, I gave birth to my last child. When she was three, I had that facial tumor removed which left half my face paralyzed for months. When I wasn't busy doing the Mom gig, or wiping drool from my own mouth, I had about a minute and a half left in the day. It took less time than that to realize I was not a happy camper.

I was busy with the kids, the house, the yard and the budget 15 to 18 hours a day, seven days a week (105 – 126 hours) while my spouse worked a measly 40 hours and spent evenings and weekends on the couch or on the golf course.

When my baby girl was almost four, I gave myself two gifts…a divorce and a boob job. (I guess that was three gifts.)

There are three reasons I'm telling you this.

1 ~ a person with half a brain could guess I've had them done, since the girls look fabulous, and...

2 ~ this is the most important, because I had it all wrong growing up. Boobs do not make the woman. You don't need big ones to be pretty, feminine, sexy or desirable. That whole story was bullshit. Once I understood this deep down inside, I realized I like me just the way I am!

What a great feeling! "Imagine," I thought to myself, "Now that I know I'm fine the way I am, how awesome it will be to have tatas with cleavage."

I got them. I did it for me and no one else. Besides, they were (and still are) more fun to look at than my crooked face.

And what is the third reason? Here it is...

3 ~ you will *never, ever* sleep on your stomach again.

It has been fifteen years and I've never regretted my implants. Right or wrong, it helped me feel better about myself, have good posture and even eat healthier.

Oh, and if anyone is rude enough to ask if my boobs are mine? I have two answers, depending on who asks and what kind of mood I'm in.

First there is the simple "yes" that goes along with a look of *I can't believe you would ask that* and then there's my favorite.

...Nope. I stole 'em!

13

Stomachs
Why Have a Flat One Anyway?

I was always so proud of my tiny waist and flat tummy that I'm working on getting it back. But I'm not working too hard. No Ab Lounger for me and I will not do 200 sit-ups like I once did, which was about the time my family got a color TV.

Instead, tending to my waistline means more veggies, less junk food and holding my stomach in. I'm telling you, if you can hold in your stomach the whole time you are doing the dishes or giving the dog a bath, you may not have a six pack, but you've got some definition going on...definition with a little cushion.

It saves time and it saves throwing out your back.

The truth is that while it may not be visually pretty, tummies are fun...especially in bed. Oh come on, let's admit it! Touching tummies with your spouse is soft, warm and tender... as long as the combined tummy size doesn't keep you from being in each other's arms. And laying your head on a soft warm tummy feels far better than a rock hard six pack.

Other Uses for Tummies:

- A breast support which keeps the twins up on the top half of the body with or without a bra.

- Saving time going through a narrow doorway. If you can't fit going forward, there's no use in turning sideways. Just go home.

- If you fall face first, the tummy gives you added time to get your hands up in case you rock forward all the way to your face.

- When playing Charades, all you have to do is poke your own tummy and your team members will instantly know it's the Pillsbury Dough Boy.

- If the dog jumps up on you, he is automatically catapulted to the sofa where you can sit on him to make him mind.

14

History of an Ass

Do you realize what a waste of time it is to hate something about yourself? Here's a case in point, my ass. Not a husband silly, the one on my backside.

I wasted years, and I can tell you exactly which ones too. From the ages of eleven to thirty years old I was embarrassed over my big round booty.

My first husband *loved* it. I thought he was lying because from its inception at eleven years old, kids had teased me unmercifully over it. They'd walk behind me and call me bubble-butt. They'd mimic how I walked as they quacked to make sure I heard them.

It wiggled and swayed. It was like sitting on a pillow everywhere I went and it was nearly impossible to find jeans to fit it. If they fit my butt, the waist was inches too big.

Husband #2 thought it was too big. He was also gracious enough to bring attention to my other hated (but matching) body part. He nick named me, *Thunder Thighs*. Sweet guy!

Husband #2 did not make me feel at all feminine or pretty. Wanting to please him (and myself) I went on a rather unhealthy diet and finally lost the thick thighs that clapped everywhere I went.

What did he say?

"Your legs look great, but what the hell happened to your ass?"

My best friend got angry. "Are you trying to kill yourself? Stop looking at your legs and look at the top half of your body! Your ribs are hanging out. God made you with strong legs and a butt. If you don't put on ten or fifteen pounds, I swear I'm going to hog tie you and force feed you grits, bacon and country ham." (She was from Virginia.)

I thought about what they both said and how this was the first time my weight was what the 'charts' said I should be. 105 pounds for my 5' frame.

I did a good long naked critique in front of the mirror. My top half looked anorexic, while the bottom half looked slender.

My ribs were nearly the size of my boobs and it hurt to sit on my bony butt.

I decided Sandra and God where right. Besides, I looked like a head on a stick. Obviously my oversized head was made to match something that was no longer there. I'm surprised I could keep the big thing on top of my neck.

For once, I asked myself the right question.

"Who devised those stupid charts anyway? A couple of drunk doctors who wanted to make females everywhere, insecure? Did they not take into consideration that muscle weighs more than fat? Maybe I just came from a dense family."

I kept exercising but gave up the 900 calories a day.

My ribs disappeared and my butt came back. I was *me* and starting to appreciate myself.

* * *

In my 30s I became proud of my butt. Okay, so I still hid my thunder thighs whenever possible. Nobody's perfect.

The truth is, I loved my 30s and 40s. Things went up and down with stress, pregnancy and a bit of laziness, but nutrition and exercise always saved the day.

My 50s got a little iffy. I kept putting off exercise. I was too busy.

Part of the problem might have been the fact that I did not own a full length mirror. My 3rd husband thought I was beautiful and sexy so I ate whatever I wanted, did not exercise for ten years and preferred our cardio enhancing sex in the dark. In other words, I hid my head in the sand.

One night I stood on the edge of the bathtub to check out my profile because it seemed my waist was becoming rather thick.

"Not too bad," I lied to myself. "After all, you are 55" (excuses, excuses).

I took out a hand held mirror to get a full rear view ...and choked.

What happened to my ass? Had someone stolen it? Had I sat too much these past ten years and crushed it? Good lord, it was a beach ball gone dead.

While it seemed to be there from my profile stance, from behind it was flat as a pancake like a victim of a sneezing ice sculptor with a chain saw.

Putting down the mirror, I joined my husband and step daughter out on the back porch.

"What's wrong baby? You look white as a ghost."

"Why didn't you tell me!" I blurted accusingly.

"Tell you what?"

"My ass is gone! I've had one my whole life, and now it's deflated, flat and ugly. It's as bad as someone shaving my head while I'm asleep. It's part of my identity."

He laughed at me. My step daughter didn't know what to make of it. She'd never had an ass anyway so she didn't know what she was missing. She looked at her dad for guidance.

I continued my lamentation, "Big booties are finally 'in' and mine took a damn hike! How can life be so, so *unfair?*"

"You're beautiful," he said in his nicest voice.

"What a liar," I thought. Was he blind? My face was getting more wrinkles by the minute and now I had been attacked and taken over by *Old Lady Butt Syndrome*. I was beside myself when I wailed, "What do I do? How do I get it back?"

He wasn't sure if this was one of those questions a wife asks that she wants an answer to, or if she's just throwing it out to the universe. Deciding to take a risk, he answered, "Squats and lunges?"

"Oh Gawd, I need a drink." I stomped off to the kitchen.

I poured myself a strong one and did a couple mini squats behind the counter where they couldn't see me. I instantly remembered how much I hated squats and lunges and wondered if my aging knees could take the punishment.

I topped off my drink, got a throw pillow and plopped it on the wrought iron deck chair when I rejoined them.

While they talked of other things, I played a self pity song in my head. As a kid I'd known one about a dog.

The lyrics were, "Where or where has my little dog gone? Where oh where can he be?"

Making it fit, I sang to myself:
Where oh where has my big booty gone,
Where oh where can it be?
With its two bulbous cheeks, and its pillow like form,
Where oh where can it be?

The sun had set. In the approaching darkness they couldn't see my teary eyes.

Young Butts

Whoever you are, whatever your age, be grateful for what you have. Focus on it, not on what you have not. I know these things, but in practice, I tend to fall off the wagon.

I look at my 19-year-old daughter with the most perfect figure I have ever seen. What does she say?

She loves her big round booty but hates her thick legs. I can't get through to her that if she had skinny legs, they'd look ridiculous with that donk.

While I look upon the girl built just like her mother, grandmother and great grandmother, I remember the words of my great grandfather (as told to me by my mother).

"I just love, love, love those wrestler's legs and the rear end that goes with them. Now, *that's* a woman!"

Then Mom would remind me that in this life, there's something for everyone. If we all looked the same, it would be boring.

Mom talked a good game but never showed her legs either. When miniskirts were popular the shortest I talked her into going was the middle of her knee.

A few months ago I noticed my daughter had lost weight. I was concerned. When I asked her about it, she admitted her father had called her fat.

I tried to stay calm. "No one with a 21 inch waist is fat."

I told her what her great-great grandfather had said and prayed I got through to her. A week later we had a big meal together (meaning she ate) and she told me she'd had a talk with her father.

Finally he acquiesced, saying, "No, you are NOT fat. You just got your mother's build and I'm afraid you're stuck with it." (He finally understood even if he never learned diplomacy.)

15

Legs Make You Taller

I am entirely grateful for all my body parts. There isn't a day that goes by I don't appreciate being able to walk but I was not in the right line when sexy legs were being handed out. And it hasn't gotten any better.

One of my own sisters was in the right line and flaunted it. Back when miniskirts were in, no one looked better than my sister. Long slender thighs, shapely calves and perfect knees is all you would see floating toward you. I considered hating her.

I wore Granny Dresses.

All four parts of her legs were perfect...thighs, knees, calves and ankles.

Everyone who knows anything about perfection knows the thighs should be 1 ¾ inches longer than the calves for the perfect ratio; be thicker than the calves and have a nice shape that blends into the butt nicely. That would be *her*.

Thighs that are 3 ¼ inches longer than the calves making the legs look like they were made from leftover parts soldered together are not pretty. Especially when they happen to be the fat storage capital of the body which makes one turn away and never want to eat cottage cheese again. Those would be mine.

Aging added stretch marks to accompany the cottage cheese making my thighs reminiscent of a relief map of Argentina.

Having thick legs is one thing but I learned a terrible truth in my 30's. When I picked up my son at daycare on my way home from work one day, the babysitter started laughing at me. I was clueless.

"What is so funny?" I asked.

"You have piano legs. I never noticed before."

"What are piano legs?"

"What? You've never heard the term? Girl, you've got no ankles. Your calves go straight to your feet."

"Of course I have ankles," I declared, and lifted up my pant leg to show her.

She laughed even harder, "No, those are definitely *not* ankles."

Not being oversensitive to the woman, I went home, promptly got pregnant, quit my job and never saw the mean old hag again.

The Poof is in the Knees

So I've always had kind of fat knees. I didn't get those cute knobby knees that other girls got and maybe they didn't like their bony knees but they were different than mine so they were cool. I wanted them. Just like the grass is always greener on the other side of the fence, the knees are always cuter on the other side of the classroom.

Everyone had knees but me.

The only way you could tell I had any was my legs

bent there. Plus there was a little dimple near the outside of each knee cap which would have been adorable on my face.

Not long ago, near the end of one of my chubbiest years, I noticed what looked like swelling just above my kneecaps. Wondering if I had water on the knee, I took a closer look.

I donned my reading glasses and held my breath since the pressure of bending at the waist made it difficult to inhale; and got good and close.

My eyes welled up with tears. It wasn't water, it was fat. My thighs were sharing the wealth.

The age monster had struck again. Either the loss of elasticity in my skin had dealt me a hefty blow by letting my thighs droop over my knees, or my double chin had fallen and split.

Either way, the result was the same. I now had double knees.

I pondered if it might be time to do something drastic.

Restless Leg Syndrome

Not long after, my legs added a new feature. They would get sore, quiver and shakes as if they had a life of their own and wanted to leave. You'd think they'd had enough of me and wanted out of the relationship. I had restless leg syndrome.

I had no idea that's what I had until I saw the commercial. The commercial said if I had shaky legs that got sore, especially at night, I had this new condition called Restless Leg Syndrome.

The drug manufacturers were on it! At the exact time I found out about it, I found out there were drugs to treat it! As my legs involuntarily quivered in front of the television, I listened to the side effects of the treatment.

After careful consideration, which took half a second, I shook my head. Rather than make the drug companies richer by taking something with side effects that would need to be treated by more drugs ...which would probably have side effects that needed to be treated by more drugs ...surely I'd use up my entire memory bank by concentrating on my pill schedule and get nothing done in life but take medication every 20 minutes of my waking hours. Plus who would pay for all this stuff?

I made a decision then and there to self treat my Restless Leg Syndrome. It's an old remedy, that's been around for years and is used to treat the following conditions.

- Restless Leg Syndrome
- Depression
- Anxiety
- Stiffness
- Aches and Pains
- Weight Gain
- Double Knees
- Double Chins
- Arm Wings
- Thunder Thighs
- Fatigue
- Mental Exhaustion
- Bad Attitude
- Poor Circulation
- Sleep Disorders
- Constipation
- Lack of Mental Focus
- Antagonistic Attitude

- Self Pity
- Junk Food Cravings
- Insecurity
- Bitchiness
- Loss of Ass
- Shopping in the Plus Sizes section

You may have heard of it. It can cost a bundle but I found a place to get it under the table for free. It's called *exercise*.

If you haven't taken it in awhile, it can be hard on the body initially but the side effects do subside all by themselves. It just takes a little longer if the only exercise you've had is scooting your desk chair around and cleaning house.

I made an error in judgment when attempting this remedy because I overdosed in the beginning.

Apparently if you haven't used this remedy in ten years, it's not a good idea to try to run two miles, no matter what you're wearing. I was gasping at an $1/8^{th}$ of a mile so decided to change it to a brisk walk. Okay, well, it was way faster than crawling and possibly brisk for a 95 year-old.

I was going as slow as molasses but I kept at it. The next day I had trouble getting out of bed, but I knew it was coming because I'd had trouble rolling over in my sleep. Actually, I don't think I even made the roll. Instead, I decided I liked the position I was in much more than I'd thought since it hurt less to stay still.

And I would have stayed in bed all day but I had to pee. Luckily, no one could see or hear me as I grunted, groaned and got myself out of the bed and did the cross country mini ski shuffle slowly to the bathroom with my back at half-mast.

Once I got on the toilet I didn't want to get up again but I couldn't stay there all day either. Obviously I needed to stretch just a tad since I'd done this drug a lot in my youth and knew the second day was always worse than the first.

I went slowly. First I shuffled into the kitchen and put on the coffee. Then I headed back to the bathroom. By the time I got there, the coffee was done but I got in the shower anyway. I needed heat for my stiffness.

I did some beginning stretches in the shower. Afterward, I leaned on the dog to get down on the floor for more stretches to loosen up everything that had turned to concrete. I made him lay next to me in case I needed help to get up.

Being the big help that he is, he laid across my stomach. I practiced shallow breathing and wriggled and stretched my feet while I waited for my 75 pound helper to scoot over.

Finally I said, "Mommy can't breathe" so he slurped my face and headed for the front door declaring potty time.

I told him his 13 year old bladder was just going to have to hold it a few minutes. Then I wondered why HE wasn't sore. I thought about the stretches he did when he got up so I mimicked him.

Luckily no one was around to see my face and chest on the floor and my ass in the air. Nearly passing out from all the blood rushing to my head, it took four century long minutes for things to stretch and reduce the stiffness enough to not look like I just got out of a body cast.

Getting up was a bit slow but I was determined to get that leash on the old man and get him out before he flooded the carpet at the front door.

The fresh air was wonderful. I felt alive and I was proud. We walked a quarter mile while I counted my blessings. One of them being gratitude that I had on tight pants or my thighs would have made the sound of thunder, making everyone in a half mile radius grab their umbrella.

My Restless Leg Syndrome was gone and now I had achy muscles. Thank god I had a reason to hurt.

When I got home I was afraid to sit down. Would everything lock up again? Does anyone make WD-40 for human joints?

I Used to Love Leather but It's All Over Now

If you never had enough leather in your wardrobe and you love the stuff, rejoice, because the grain of leather will be imparted on your legs.

It varies from woman to woman, how healthy you've eaten and how much sun you've baked under, but somewhere in the fifties you notice a grain to your calves. It varies from barely discernible crackle lines to the parched, cracked soil at the end of a ten year drought.

Whatever you do, keep your arms away from your legs! The lower arms get jealous of the new look and just have to have it and next thing you know, you're drinking buckets of water since your skin reminds you of something between the Sahara Desert and Kenya during the dry season.

Lotions do not help. Being dipped in paraffin wax helps for 20 minutes and now I'm working on a new cure. Cold pressed coconut oil. I'll let you know how it goes.

What I know so far is, do not use it if you have brittle bones. I'll get to the 'why' in a minute. Organic cold pressed coconut oil is a very healthy fat to eat, treat dry skin and as a weight loss aid.

So I decided to slather up my legs and arms and everything in between to get gorgeous and healthy. Besides I wouldn't miss my thunder thighs or my arm wings so it was worth a try.

Could there be a downside to coconut oil?

I was so excited when I found the stuff at the grocery store. As soon as I got home, I opened the jar and disrobed.

It smelled great but looked like Crisco shortening. My reading retention being short, I just took it a step at a time, about a sentence worth.

It's a solid and the instructions say to put the jar in warm water to liquefy. I didn't want to wait so I dug a chunk out of the jar and melted it by rubbing my hands together.

So far so good, except the phone rang. I looked from my greasy hands to my cell phone and back again. I grabbed a pen and pushed the answer button and then the speaker button.

"Hello?"

"What's up", said my eldest?

"I'm standing here naked about to put coconut oil all over me to get rid of my wrinkles."

"Oh, God, call me later." Click. The boy has no sense of humor.

After slathering up all my dry parts I felt like a grease ball but I smelled totally tropical. Then I read the next part. Keep it on for an hour to give it time to soak in.

I couldn't stay naked an hour! Someone might see me or I might break a mirror. Never mind I was alone. When you're naked in the middle of the day you just feel totally self conscious, like someone might be watching.

It's not like anyone would want to, it's just a glitch in mental makeup. I thought I might feel more comfortable sitting down.

After sliding off the kitchen chair, the sofa, and the bed; I got bored standing around naked. Besides, there was just too much air flow. I'd never be able to go to a nudist colony because my body was going into shock from all the fresh air.

Then the dog discovered I was wearing coconut oil and thought it was awesome. He decided to clean me up. I told him no and shooed him away, but he insisting I needed help.

When he got one lick in above the knee, I went into embarrassment mode; jiggled and slid down the hall, grabbed my robe and hid inside it. It became a race between my skin and the robe as to who was going to absorb more coconut oil. I had to wait it out to see who would win.

I looked at the clock and there was 50 minutes to go so I set about cleaning the faux leather sofa, kitchen chair and threw my sheets in the washer.

I sat on the sofa with a book and fell asleep while the grease soaked into the pages. Ninety minutes later I awoke shocked that I was no longer greasy and my skin was oh-so-soft.

Hopefully after a few more treatments, my skin won't look like my favorite purse. Pleased as punch, I ran my hands up and down my calves and smiled ...until I saw my feet.

16

Feet and Piggly Wigglies

I have never met anyone who liked their own feet. If you do, send me a picture with proof it's you and I'll post it on Facebook.

Honestly, where do they get those foot models? Perfect toe length, perfect nail size and not one of those little piggies is crooked. That's just not natural.

I've had ugly feet since I was a kid. It was always kind of up for grabs whether my second piggy is longer than the big girl who went to market. The fact is, the only reason the big girl went to market in the first place was to get chocolate. She got depressed that her sisters were all so much thinner and chocolate was the only thing that eased the pain. Besides, she always had to stand next to the tallest and thinnest of the siblings.

The piggy that stayed home is tall and slender and the tip of her is reminiscent of a used balloon. You know, the ones that clowns make weenie dogs out of, except that it got blown up too many times. She's long and skinny with a little ball on the end. She blames this on the gal who had roast beef not giving her enough room. I have a sneaky suspicion she has an oversized head like me.

The gal who had roast beef (#3) is shaped like a backwards C as though the tall slender balloon-head forgot deodorant. She's doing her best to stay away.

Now if you take a look at #4, maybe she had no roast beef because she had no room. Did anyone think of that? When she's packed in tight with her sisters, she looks okay, but if I spread my toes, she falls over in a heap. Sad! It looks like she's down for the count.

Then we have the last little piggy who ran wee-wee-wee so fast, that she hardly has a nail bed on her piggy head. It either flew off somewhere in her travels or was knocked against the coffee table one too many times by her sisters who wanted to give her something to cry about since she's a whiner anyway.

And that's just the right foot! The left foot is in worse shape. Heaven help me.

So I'm not fond of my feet. Not a real big deal since pretty feet are few and far between and shoes were invented to cover ugly feet. Later shoes became a way to warp piggies. Add calluses and bunions to the mix, in an effort to slow us down when chasing our husbands to give them a piece of our mind.

Not that they don't need it, but because it's better we keep our minds for ourselves. If we give our minds to our spouses, they won't use them anyway.

Of course feet look best in the winter when they are covered with shoes or trendy boots, but year after year summer returns. This means a three month beautification process. The older I get, the earlier in the season I have to start the process.

Never mind I have to keep the nails a tad bit long in sandal weather so it appears I have nail beds. I have kept them painted in lovely colors religiously since I was a ten and I vow to until my dying day.

I figure it looks better, plus it's great exercise both physically and mentally. I put on my reading glasses; hoist my foot up on the same chair my ass occupies and see how many toes I can paint before my breath runs out, my leg cramps or my glasses fall off my face and land in fresh toenail polish.

As far as life's challenges, this one is small patooties.

While you're painting your toes, do NOT look at your heels like I did. If you do, you will immediately understand why you get runs in your pantyhose on those rare occasions you decide to wear them.

Your heels have turned to pumice! The skin is so tough you could walk a field of broken glass without bleeding if you could just balance on the right spot.

Pumice stones with wrinkles above them. Is God laughing at me yet? I hope so because one of us should be laughing.

I tried using a pumice stone on my heels but I couldn't tell which was wearing down faster - the stone or my heels. Now twice a year I get a pedicure to get ready for the warm season. The women who beautify my feet use something like an oversized cheese grater on my heels and scrape them right over a dust pan for quick removal.

I swear I'm a decent tipper; especially if they can get through it without making a face. I'm a little iffy when a gal in her 20's looks at me as if it's *my fault* my feet look like this.

When it happens, I just smile and think, "You just wait girlie, because your day will come."

And every year they tell me my heels look like this because I don't get pedicures often enough. Give me a break. In three days, it'll look like I've never been there.

Besides, I don't have the patience to sit in a salon that often twiddling my thumbs.

If I had a laptop I could get some work done while the pedicure was taking place ...unless I got a foot cramp, which does happen. I've played this scenario in my head where I get one and drop my laptop into the tub of skin filled water.

The foot cramps aren't as bad as the toe cramps though because one can *see* the toe cramps. I swear the pedicurist looks at me like I'm doing it on purpose.

It's always toe #2; you know the one who stayed home? Obviously, she's not used to getting out because she'll go stiff and look cock-eyed like she's trying to roll over and play dead. I wonder if that's the real reason feet are called dogs.

The unnatural look is bad enough but when she starts to quiver, it hurts like a son of a gun and I look away as if I don't notice ...while the entire time I'm gritting my dentures so hard I'm afraid they'll shatter.

Now that we've established my dogs are tired, to top it off my toes are now wrinkled. First I noticed the lines that ran across my toes were hanging around even after a toe cramping episode.

Then, like a fool, I looked at my feet with my glasses on and found the area between those big wrinkles looks like I poured that antiquing glaze on them I used on the furniture so I had something that looked older than I do.

Just talking about toe wrinkles makes me long for pregnancy in my 30's when my feet had no wrinkles whatsoever. My edema was so bad I made Fred Flintstone's feet look slender and shapely.

...Ah, the good old days.

So bless your feet. Even if they look like rough leather that wasn't tanned well, not only do they do the walking thing like nobody's business, they are a great support and keep you balanced.

Why don't we move on to…

Book Two

~*~

Life's Little Experiences

17

Bodily Functions

Shall we speak of gas? What is the big damn deal with farting? My kids don't hold back. Why is it such a source of embarrassment for me? Of course it never helped that one of my ex-husbands used to fart in public and blame it on me. I can't believe he lasted 18 years. I swear if I wasn't pregnant the first time he pulled that on me, I would have been gone like the wind. (Am I funny or what?)

After that, I never laughed when he blamed it on the dog. Instead I gave the dog pizza. If you ever want to make someone leave your house, just give your dog a piece of pizza and close the windows.

Thank god my cat pooped on him while he was sleeping in the guest room or I never would have gotten rid of the man.

Now, my mother had dignity and very good manners. I never ever heard that woman fart. She taught me the four rules of farting.

- Hold it and release it slowly and gently so no one

can hear it.
- Hold it and leave the room. Find a place where you can be alone and let it go.
- If you suspect it will be a stinker, take the trash out or pretend there is something important to do outside.
- If you happen to release the silent but deadly variety, light a match and fan the area like crazy so anyone walking in the room once you leave, will not know. (Something about the sulfur in the match tip.)

While the rest of the world seems to have no problem with this bodily function while around others, I do. Even if I do the hold and release slowly method, my face turns red. This is not from concentration, it is from embarrassment. Everyone who knows me... knows when I fart. Does this make me the butt of my kids' jokes? Naw! Now that they're grown they just think I'm cute. Imagine hearing, "Mom, you are SO cute!" I think they say that so I stay red longer. It works.

Fart Facts

Okay, these may not be facts, just my opinion but there are several types of farts and often very specific causes.

Food Combo Flatulence – This isn't good. I'm using the older generation's definition of sick. (Meaning it's gross, not great.) They smell awful and the tummy rumbles loudly in between. They can be caused by the wrong mix of food and drink. An example would be: Pizza, beer, hot wings, potato skins, onion rings and topped off with a few margaritas. Not only do you feel sick, but anyone who smells your stuff feels sick as well.

Fast Food Farts do not have alcohol mixed with them and usually can be achieved by one visit to McDonalds. Quarter pounder with cheese anyone? I listed McDonalds first because at this point in my life, all I have to do is drive by the place and my tummy rumbles. If I ever get a hankering for Micky D's I better have a full tank of gas (in the car silly) because I have to drive around for quite some time before I go shopping or go home. After all, I must maintain some of my dignity.

Taco Bell is actually my favorite fast food and likely the only one I will eat nowadays. Still, if I don't stick to two plain tacos I'm in trouble. I know meat AND beans don't digest well together once we're past the age of about 22 but every now and then I feel a need to test my theory with a burrito supreme.

This is a deadly combo and not recommended in winter months when you can't roll down the car windows since odiferous flatulence begins within four minutes of the last swallow of a burrito supreme.

Burger King went downhill once they stopped the flame broiling thing, plus I have trouble finding the burger in the bun now. Either their food got worse or my tolerance did. Still, my daughter loves the place so we go when we're together and I can roll down the window.

If Crystals is not in your neck of the woods, don't feel bad. I'd rather starve than eat there unless I'm so famished I'm not thinking about the stomach ache that follows.

They have these mini burger type things with surprise meat. Personally when I ate there I actually prayed for gas hoping to relieve my stomach ache. (If you work for Crystals Corporate, let's say this is a joke so you don't sue me. You can't get blood out of a turnip anyway.) And the only reason I didn't mention White Castle is I've never been there. I hear it's the Northern version of Crystals.)

Baby Farts come in two categories. The farts that babies make are cute but then everything babies do is adorable. Come on, even when they scrunch up their face to pass something, you can't help but smile unless you are a new father with poop phobia left alone with your baby for the first time. (I will cover that in my second book *Put Down the Damn Toilet Seat*).

The other baby farts are similar to walking farts but quieter. They can be sneaky and one can be unaware of their presence. I found out about baby farts from my husband. No, no, no, he doesn't do them. Everything he does is big because he's very macho. Apparently its ME!

After five years of marriage he finally told me that I fart in my sleep. This meant to me that I'd lost control. He swore it was very cute and he couldn't believe anyone could make such tiny quiet farts. He swears it sounds like a putt-putt noise with a long pause in the middle. Obviously my fart control during slumber needs work.

Walking farts are something I've heard of but thankfully not experienced. They seem to pass with each step someone takes. I can't believe they are a sign of age like Larry the Cable Guy says, but I can attest to the fact that two of my dogs get them on a regular basis. It's pretty funny to see a dog stop and sniff her own butt to see what's going on back there, as if it were some outside source.

I'll have to get out the movie camera next time. Dog farting is cute like baby farting. Adult humans should know better.

(Update) On Tuesday I had the walking farts. I was minding my own business at the Mall. My daughter and I were sipping on our Starbucks Mocha coffees and chatting when all of a sudden; putt-putt-putt. This stopped my daughter dead in her tracks.

"Mom!"

Shocked and red faced, I answered, "I'm never listening to Larry the Cable Guy again. This is *his* fault. I never even heard of walking farts before he came along. Since thoughts are things, he made me manifest farts. I need to go home."

Sneaky farts are the worst! They come out of nowhere and they are not quiet. Without warning, they sneak right on out and announce themselves with gusto. If there is a cure, please email me. I've done that twice in 57 years! (Now I have to up that number to three if I count those walking ones.)

Not Farts. You know what this is. A little pressure in the abdomen that you are sure will go away if you just give it a little helpful push. The second you start to give it some help, your eyes get wide, you scrunch up your butt and get to the toilet ASAP. A close call every time. Of course this has never happened to me.

Farting Styles

Recently my daughter and I took a three day road trip to get her dog back from her step dad. Twenty four hundred miles in three days was quite a trek. We stopped to sleep twice but other than that, it was gas and snack foods and gas.

Meaning, we stopped to fill the car's gas tank several times and ate snack foods so we could keep driving. The snack foods in turn, being somewhat short of nutrition, created the other type of gas.

In the middle of the second day I caught a whiff of something ...and knew darn well it wasn't the dog in the back seat.

"Sweetheart, did you just fart?"

"It's nice of you to ask. Why yes I did."

"Well, while you may not think it smells bad, I do. For heaven's sake, have the decency to roll down the window."

Next thing you know, we're discussing flatulence. Those that blame; those who somehow find pride in the act; and low and behold positions folks use to let go.

The stay-sitting fart is for folks who prefer to muffle it and keep it trapped as long as possible so no one else notices; alas, gas rises so this is a very temporary method for non disclosure.

The single cheek lift style. If you are left handed you lift the right butt cheek; right handed, the left cheek. (Unless I have that backwards.) There is everything from the unnoticeable lift to the full fledged lift that looks like you're going to aim it at someone.

The cheek lift is supposed to make the exit of gas a more pleasant experience by unblocking the pathway.

If used at a park bench, for instance, the smell dissipates almost immediately if there is a breeze.

The full bottom lift style. I've never quite understood this one. I'm not sure if the slight lifting of the entire buttocks is suppose to be less noticeable or; whether it's a thigh exercise or folks who use this one are afraid of falling over using the single cheek lift.

The only one I know who uses this style is anally retentive so why he lets it loose at all is a wonder.

The Ben Dover. For tricksters and those who aim, the Ben Dover (bend over) helps get that gas near the exit. It's the ready; aim; fire method of farting and is usually used against the dog because dogs won't fart fight.

The bath tickle. Loved by females everywhere, lying in the tub and letting go is nearly soundless and tickles as it heads for the surface. The fight to get through the water renders these feminine farts almost non aromatic. Hmm, maybe not!

The dog fart. As the name implies, this occurs when the dog farts. I've even seen guilty human gas passers use the first step of this ritual to feign innocence.

First, there is a putt-putt sound emanating from the canine's posterior. The dog then looks both ways to see where it came from as if it were an uninvited intruder.

While some dogs end it there, most inquisitively give their rear end a few sniffs and cock their head as if to say, "For heaven's sake, what was that?"

I know an adorable Pomeranian who does this but ends it by running like the devil is chasing her and hides under the bed. Once the dog takes off, her owners know to leave the room as well.

Unnatural Acts on the Commode

My last husband did the same thing my father did. Smell up the bathroom and then leave for work. There should be a law against that. Come on, even the dogs laid on the sofa with their paws over their nose. It was cruel.

After my father retired, moved away, and came back to visit; my sisters would fight over where Daddy was going to stay. Everyone loved his company but running the fan for an hour after he'd used the commode, didn't seem to help much, and who wants to open all the windows and doors in the middle of winter?

Bodily functions get louder and stink more with age. Why is that? Did all that fast food catch up with us and wear us out? Did it make our spouses lose their hearing? Really, did my spouse think no one could hear the noises he was making in the bathroom? It sounded like he was dying in there.

And how can anyone use an entire roll of toilet paper in one sitting and NOT think the toilet will back up. With this husband I had to leave a plunger next to the toilet at all times.

Not that he was going to use it. He'd feign ignorance; leave on the light, the fan, close the bathroom door and sneak off to work.

I'd go in later to find something still floating. "Good grief," I'd think, "How hard is it to flush?"

I'd flush.

My anger would then rise along with the toilet water ...and the race was on. I'd hold my breath and bend down to reach the toilet water supply. Would I get it shut it off before my feet got wet? I wanted to squeal like a girl and call him at work to cuss him out.

What a wonderful way to start the day.

* * *

I on the other hand, am a very conscientious and appreciative pooper. Normal pooping is a joy. Not only do you feel a pant size smaller, you now have room to eat again! And let's face it; eating is fun stuff... as long as your teeth stay in.

Of course, we'd all rather do it in the privacy of our own home, but it's not always possible. Especially if you stopped for fast food en route to the mall.

You're shopping a great sale and need to make a surprise trip to the ladies room. Talk about embarrassment! And who designs public restrooms anyway? The acoustics amplify every fart and anything that hits the water sounds like you just did the high dive in a swimming competition.

Here's a scenario. You rush (with dignity) to the ladies room and there are other women in there. You try your best to poop quietly but it sounds like someone is shooting your grandson's super soaker against an aluminum trash can lid.

This is where you hate whoever designed women's restrooms.

So there you are trying to be quiet and you can't. When you're done and want to run because you didn't bring a gas mask with you; realization sets in. If it smells terrible to YOU, how does it smell to others? Come on, it has got to be worse. You know it and I know it.

If you walk out now, what if you come face to face with someone who you'll see again in the sweater section? You just know she'll give you such a disgusted look you couldn't bear it. And she's probably shopping with her best friend and she's going to whisper to her friend while staring you down.

Now what? There's only one thing to do.

You listen, waiting for everyone to leave.

You can't tell whether someone just went out or someone just came in. In the meantime you're getting light headed from holding your breath while you wish to God they had an exhaust fan in this place.

You don't know whether to make a run for it or just walk out looking innocent. After all, the smell must now encompass at least three stalls.

You are having trouble thinking and you fear you'll pass out, fall off the toilet, be discovered and someone will take your picture with their iPhone and post it on Facebook. They'll say what you did. It'll go viral and get 1,000,000 views.

Not only will you have to change your Facebook

avatar to the dog's picture, you can never leave your house again.

Or maybe someone has already taken a picture of your shoes from outside the stall. What then?

It finally gets quiet. You peek out. Either no one else shopping for women's clothes during this 50% off sale has to go to the bathroom (fat chance) or you've scared them off.

You wash your hands and go straight to the shoe section praying for a pair you like to be on sale.

You find them, but you are near enraged that the only pair you find worth having are a mere 20% off. You know that's hardly sale material and feel totally taken advantage of by the store and their sales ad.

You are about to put them back on the sales rack and leave the store in disgust when you simultaneously see a rack of sweaters for 75% off and recognize a voice from the bathroom.

You drop the shoes to the floor, schooch into them and put the shoes you were wearing in the bathroom in the new shoe box and tuck them under your arm.

You head for the sweater rack while trying to decide to actually buy the shoes on your feet or sneak them back on the sales rack before you leave the store.

I'm guessing men don't think this way.

* * *

I once overheard my son and a friend talking about taking a dump. Before I tell you the story, I've got to ask something. Who on earth coined this phrase? I've never taken a dump anywhere. Nor have I taken a turd. Who started this crap?

This is something my sixty-something year old sister

still says. I hate it. Every time she says it in my presence, I ask her where she took it. We butt heads quite a bit. Mom said she'd get over it 40 years ago, but I'm tired of waiting.

Anyway, let's get back to my son. God knows I love the guy but I'm worried about his sex life. I don't have the nerve to ask him or his wife but this is just part of a conversation I heard several years ago (God I hope it's gotten better)

(Son) "There is nothing better than taking a dump. It has got to be the best feeling in the world."

(Son's Friend) "No kidding. It's totally orgasmic and completely underrated."

(Son) "It could be better than sex."

I've never brought up what I overheard but I'm still waiting for grandchildren.

Belching & Burping

I see these as two different things. Burps can be sneaky and the volume is lower than a belch. As long as you keep your mouth closed and put your hand over it to muffle the sound further, you're good to go. I am queen at burp muffling.

Belching is an entirely different matter. It's horrendously loud and sounds like you've been storing a bomb in your belly.

What's worse is talking to a man who, in the middle of a sentence, opens his mouth wide and let's out something that sounds like it could take out New York City. He'll ignore the experience, not excuse himself and just keep on talking. That would be my third husband.

I will give him credit for waiting nine years before he

broke the belch-o-meter but it kind of pissed me off. Why did he lose respect for me?

He knew how I felt. Still, belching seems to be a guy thing that starts in grade school.

* * *

I remember watching my sons with their friends. They would sit around doing whatever it took to produce belches and outdo each other.

At the kitchen table they would chug a coke to get a few good ones going until they mastered the air swallow. To young boys it appears to be an art form.

Either some guys don't grow out of it, don't notice it or don't care.

When my husband started belching in front of me, I was surprised. If I brought it up, he often denied it. I took it as he didn't care if I stayed or left.

The day he rattled my eardrum by belching into the phone was the day I hung up on him.

He called back and asked what was wrong.

When I told him I was totally grossed out at his 'f-you' attitude by belching in my ear, he swore he did not belch in the phone. This is the same guy who swore he made the house payments.

Yeah, right.

If you can get your three aunts, fourteen cousins and 1042 friends on Facebook to buy this book I can finally serve him papers.

If you really want to be supportive, you can write a review on Amazon saying how witty and charming I am in this book which will earn my undying gratitude and appreciation.

I just realized I should write a book titled "The Man

Book" to make fun of those we love because there's so much more to say that doesn't quite fit in this one. I'll put it on my to-do list right now. Right after the divorce and I get my sense of humor back.

My next man will be a dog. They may bark but they don't belch or clog the toilet.

18

Female Fashions
If it's Not Comfortable, Wear It

Female clothing fashions change so fast it's hard to keep up and sometimes I just don't care. Once you've lived long enough to see a few styles come around again, you realize it's all pretty silly.

It would be a lot more fun if fashion was comfortable and either hid body flaws or at least accentuated our least offensive features.

Case in point, the current style of wearing clothes five sizes too small (unless it's ten). On a gal who's in shape? Not bad as long as she doesn't mind looking naked covered with sausage skin.

How about anyone with a body flaw? Dear god, I want to run and throw a blanket over them. How can you even hold a conversation with someone who's got a pierced flabby abdomen that jiggles while she speaks, or her shirt keeps creeping into her folds?

I loved the long soft flowing dresses and skirts with

boots or bare feet and ankle jewelry in San Francisco back in the era of Bill Graham's Filmore and Winterland concerts, when 'hippie' was cool. *That* was feminine. When the style faded, I was sorely disappointed.

I made the switch to jeans and t-shirts. Like most females (I think) the last style you wore in high school sticks like glue. I'll know for sure, if my daughter is still wearing glued on clothes ten years from now that appear toddler size before she squeezes into them.

My basic jeans held for years. Eventually I threw out the t-shirts and used anything from tank tops to turtlenecks to shear soft feminine blouses (with camisoles underneath, because I am silly and do not want to appear half naked when not at the beach).

Then something happened to change me forever. I discovered jeans with spandex. The stretch made me feel so free! I could actually bend and my pants stayed with me.

Not long after that (when I was 55) I realized I didn't need the jeans at all. What a concept!

While I adore soft stretchy clothes, there is a difference between my daughter and I. When mine come out of the dryer, they look maybe a size smaller than I am. But my daughters? I swear they can get lost in the lint filter and fit a Barbie doll.

Her pants on the fanny area are so tight you can see her skin and butt crack. Her tops are often snug, causing boobage overflow reminiscent of a Pillsbury Crescent Rolls package with the strip peeled off and just banged against the counter.

My pants are just snug enough to slow down the jiggles from no longer running regularly. My tops are not tight and I prefer to keep the twins to myself.

I don't know how she even breathes in her clothes but

the one thing we agree on is this. Once you've had soft stretchy clothes you never want to go back.

And the *soft* has become a must. I bet we'd be a hoot to watch clothes shopping.

She looks first, and feels after. I feel first and then look. I'm not sure if we appear to be stealing or just molesting, but we make clothes hunting a very tactile affair.

"Oh my god, did you feel this one?"

"Ah, I know! Too bad it's ugly."

"I know! I would have bought one in every color."

"Ooh, those sweaters look soft over there."

"You're right! I'll race you."

"I am too dignified for that. Run by me so I can trip you and get there first."

We also adore any kind of makeup we can try for a buck. It could be why she has 14 pounds of makeup and needs an entire chest of drawers for the stuff.

I on the other hand, have better sense. If I don't love it, I give it to her so if I change my mind and want to retry something, I know just where to find it.

Let's get back to clothing. I'm thrifty by nature. I can't help it. My parents grew up in the Great Depression. I can find soft things anywhere. Sales racks, including Walmart and even thrift stores.

Once I've saved a ton by buying a dozen things for a dollar each, I feel rich and ready to pay full price for something on the next outing. Isn't twelve bucks full price?

Maybe my pricing guideline is outdated, but twelve bucks was a shit load when I was in junior high. It so upset me, I started sewing all my own clothes. I don't know but maybe I got stuck in some kind of space/price continuum.

All I know is that I choose what looks good on me (or at least not bad if it makes me feel good.)

Sometimes You Have to Look in the Mirror

I think I'm entering a new clothes crisis era, but this time it's a good one since I lost 40 pounds. (This happened slowly during the teeth and exercise experiences.) I have to find clothing that looks good on me, for my current figure and weight, regardless of fashion. I keep fashion in mind but I don't let it dictate.

While my poor ass is gone and my tummy is bigger than in my youth, the girls still stand strong. I'm toying with the idea of going back to the long flowing skirts but making them current with belts, tops and boots. Wish me luck.

If I get famous I might make the ten worst dressed list, but I'll be comfy!

Underwear and Where Did They Go?

What on earth happened to underwear? I love the current selection of bras. Thousands of styles whether basic, sexy, sport or bra bands. Still, the object is to cover the breasts; help them look better, feel better or run without knocking yourself unconscious.

So what, pray tell, is the point of panties? I thought they were supposed to keep private parts from making clothes dirty before their time. You know, keep clothes from, uh, spots and odors.

I could understand panties getting smaller if it was saving the rain forest, but truly I don't see the point in wearing something that doesn't do anything but go up your butt.

Yes, I'm talking about **the thong**...a middle aged woman's nightmare. In this instance, wearing clean underwear in case you get in an accident has no value whatsoever since they *don't cover anything* and certainly can't hold anything.

All they do is send you little messages each time you move. "Ooh, I'm up your butt" or "Warning, warning. Camel toe"!

Get serious. I don't want to be constantly fooling with my crotch because my panties won't stay in the panty place.

My daughter swears they're comfortable and wouldn't wear anything else. I have tried and I can honestly say after owning 37 pair of thongs, I had only one pair that stayed where I put them with a crotch wide enough to actually cover my hunanny without diving into it and getting lost.

Even those eventually stretched out and the fit was lost ...so I'm back to those humungous old fashioned bikinis. I just wish my daughter could see the kind of panties I was brought up wearing.

Remember those? They were just called panties and covered your entire ass, any part in the front that might have pubic hair, a happy trail or a belly button. Geez, my daughter could cut a hole in the crotch of one of those and wear it as a frigging nightgown.

So now let's get down to pricing. We have 1/18th of the material it took to make panties, but the price is higher? Oh come on! I can still buy big bikinis for less than my kid pays for thongs and BOTH of them will go up your butt depending on the fit.

I could probably buy the old fashioned panties for the same price but I wouldn't be caught dead looking at them. I only know one person left on the entire planet that still wears those things and I'm keeping it a secret. Poor thing!

Life is too short to be uncomfortable. As far as I'm concerned, only two things are worth physical pain. Since we're talking about thongs, I'll admit there is one pair I wouldn't mind getting as a gift. The Victoria Secret diamond studded thong. It would have to hurt, but I wouldn't mind someone saying I had diamonds up the ass. I bet even my Yaya would have liked that.

* * *

My daughter actually said this...

"Mom, I got these panties on sale for 99 cents and I love them. (she holds up a speck of lace) Have you ever seen anything so pretty? Anyway, when I washed them they shrunk. Now they're so small they make my butt cheeks look fabulous by my crotch looks like a camel dying of heat stroke."

How Could I Forget Shoes?

The perfect pair of shoes is worth the physical pain. While any shoes could be uncomfortable, in this category high heels reign supreme. Just seems to me, if you're going to hurt, it should be because your new height makes your weight look better. Let's face it, 130 pounds on a 5' frame is fatter than 130 pounds on stilettos or even better, platforms. Now we're looking at 5'4" or 5'6". I feel thinner just thinking about it.

And I learned early on how to rotate shoes so each day a different part of my foot hurt on weekdays when I wore heels. On the weekends I went barefoot to recover and get ready for the next workweek where I would look fabulous.

I sometimes wonder if I'm kin to Dolly Parton. I love that woman's shoes and I still seek out platforms whenever possible. I even wore them to my son's wedding for the first nine hours of festivities. After dancing and drinking however, I decided to 'go fat'. Not only did my feet hurt, I had just explained to someone what cow tipping was and I didn't like the look in his eyes.

I could never bond with another woman who didn't love shoes. It's like a man who doesn't love cars. It's just not natural.

Can a woman have too many pairs of shoes? I doubt it. Okay, Imelda Marcus may have hit the mark back in the day with the tally of 3,000 pair.

Still you have to give the woman credit. Out of 3,000 pair she only left 1,220 behind in 1986 when she and her husband, Dictator Ferdinand Marcus, fled the Philippines during the people's revolt.

How on earth did she choose? Did she go by color, style or did she just grab all the ones she hadn't worn yet? When you're fleeing a country who the hell carries them out for you?

If you ever visit Manila in the Philippines, you can still see 800 pair in her shoe museum for just P50 per person.

I probably won't be heading in that direction anytime soon but I may go back to Dollywood in Pigeon Forge, Tennessee. Not only is it my favorite amusement park, I can visit a few pair of Dolly's shoes to get my fix.

Dogs and Shoes

How far would I go to protect my shoes? I'm not sure. My first ever dog had a chewing stage that left me weeping. Apparently my shoes had a special place in her heart as well, since she preferred them over her chew toys when I was at work.

The worst day of my life (I was young then) was when she chose to dine on one of my most expensive shoes of all time.

At 18, it had taken me nearly three months to pay for them using the store's lay-away plan and I'd only worn them twice. I must have kept that one lonely unchewed, blue suede high heel sandal for a year, just because it was so pretty. (Okay, maybe three. It was gorgeous.)

I later realized she really did love shoes because she'd only nibbled on them. How did I know the difference? Once my shoes were unavailable, she chewed half of a brick off the fireplace hearth. Apparently, Great Danes have a lot of jaw power to go with those indestructible teeth.

While I realize there are more important things in life than shoes (like teeth and maybe my health) I think I can honestly say if there had been a house fire back then I'd have yelled at Gretchen to get out, opened a window and started tossing out shoes like mad. I had very little furniture but I had 32 pairs of shoes, and I was proud. At eighteen, that was status!

Many years later I was the laughing stock of the household when I found a chewed up boot inside my Pit Bull Helen's crate. Normally very patient with my dogs, I lost control and wanted to whoop the dog's ass.

What was so funny about it is she knew exactly what I wanted to do and hunkered in the back of that huge crate and wouldn't come out. She had braced herself inside the thing so well that when I tried pulling her out by her collar, the entire kennel went sliding around the living room floor while my husband and son laughed uproariously.

Are There Any Shoes I Won't Wear?

Absolutely! My daughter wears flat boots. I didn't even know they made boots without heels. What's the point? Still after seeing her in them for a few years, the look has grown on me.

Will I ever wear them? Nope. Maybe it's the voice of husband #2. I still hear him in my head saying, "Oh my god, without heels on, it's obvious you need shin implants. The bottom half of your leg is so short!" Even after I insisted I had long thighs, it didn't matter. The damage had been done.

You will never see me in a pair of Birkenstocks either. Those have got to be the ugliest things in the world. One of my sisters has one pair for her entire wardrobe and I can't believe we are related. Even my Yaya would not approve of wearing something like that out of the house.

I once tried on a pair in the store when no one was looking. Everyone who wears Birkies, raves about the comfort. Obviously those who wear them do not have flat feet because those suckers hurt.

What they call arch support feels like a concrete wedge. Plus all the weight was on my heels making my toes feel airborne and balancing a task.

Pointy Toed Shoes

Well darn, you won't catch me wearing these shoes either. First of all, it's more fun to pass a kidney stone that wear something that squeezes your toes into a point.

It doesn't help at all to buy them a half size bigger to give your toes room because then your heel just slips out while your toes get wedged in the tight little pointy area.

And have you ever seen someone's feet who wore pointed shoes long term? God bless my Yaya. She looked like a queen when she went out, but at home? When she took her shoes off, her feet were still pointed.

My feet aren't exactly beautiful but I am not adding bunions to the list of complaints.

Do I Ever Wear Flat Shoes?

Funny you should ask. The answer is yes. Since there's some stupid rule about not allowing heels on the tennis court, I had no choice at all. And was I shocked to find really comfortable tennis shoes weren't cheap!

Comfortable tennis shoes get pretty pricey and since my spouse number two wouldn't let me take it out of the grocery money, it ruined my shoe budget for months.

I was so mad, I got cross trainers so I could play tennis and run in the same shoes. Then I beat his ass in San Francisco's Bay to Breakers 10K race. Heck, never mind the shoe budget! It was worth it to beat him after he gave me the nick name, "Thunder Thighs." Ass hole!

19

Body Hair and the Great Migration

Hey, is this just me? I'm having trouble finding the humor in my eyesight going down the tubes before my body hair was done migrating.

I know I've covered the eyebrow debacle and unruly nose hair but what about the rest of it. Good grief. I lose it in one place only to have it sprout up somewhere else even less appropriate.

I can't tell whether the stuff is moving east, west or just south.

As a kid the hair on my arms was dark. It was embarrassing but livable. Then a lot of it migrated to a smaller central location. My arm pits. I pretty much expected that.

My arm pits still need daily shaving to keep a semblance of order and protection from being stabbed to death by straight hairs the size and strength of porcupine quills. That too, I can deal with far better than the eyebrows that moved to the mustache zone. Luckily, razors are stronger now.

Mustaches

Everyone who goes through menopause has a mustache. It helps take the eyes off the earth's gravitational pull of the boobs. However, some of us don a "stache" at earlier age, especially those of us with a Mediterranean heritage.

My brother who became my sister (a rather long story) insisted I get electrolysis to free me of my unsightly mustache when I was 25. Heck back then it was hardly noticeable.

Once her electrolysis was completed and she'd been on hormone therapy for a few years, she had less facial hair than I and a bigger chest. Life seemed so unfair.

Electrolysis not in the budget, I had to use other options.

Plucking didn't take too long before the age of 45 and lasted longer. After that, a problem developed. The problem was…missing the pluck!

Yup! If you've ever had to pluck without your reading glasses, you probably know what I'm talking about. Oh, Gawd! It hurts to grab hold of your skin with the tweezers, right under the nose. Makes your eyes water and leaves a red spot that looks like you just picked a gargantuan pimple.

How unfair is that? To finally be old enough to not have pimples anymore and then look like you spent the morning working on one? Not cool. I seem to scar more easily now.

Of course I could have it waxed but I'd have to grow

it out first. This seems a rather high price to pay. Plus I'm a little bit scared to do it.

Why? My upper lip is rather sensitive. I once got the bright idea to use a cream hair remover on it just before a party I threw. Why I thought it would only remove the hair is beyond me. My skin was beet red for the party. It resembled bad sunburn with tiny blisters.

Being too late to cancel the party I tried to ignore it. It drew so much attention I had to admit what I did. Not the party talk I was anticipating, but I was very popular.

The Great Migration of Thigh Hair

My thighs have changed so much I don't know what to expect next. I used to shave them along with the rest of my legs a few times a week. In my thirties the hair was so light and sparse on my thighs that I no longer had to shave them. Thrilled, I appreciated the time it saved to cut them out of the shaving ritual.

Then my thigh hair took a trip and sprouted on my toes. This was less than feminine and it took practice to shave the little round things without nicking them and having to put little pieces of toilet paper on those annoying little wounds. (You know, I never understood that toilet paper thing. The minute you take off the paper you just bleed all over again.)

My thighs didn't act up again until my mid forties when my oldest was a full-fledged teenager.

On a hot humid Southern summer day, I had just packed up the car with everything the kids and I would need to go swimming. I had no problem wearing a swimsuit then since I was running 10 – 12 miles a week and exercising as well.

Rounding up the threesome, my eldest said I wasn't ready.

I didn't get it. I was standing there in my swimsuit, holding my towel. "Of course I'm ready. Let's go."

"Mom," he said, "I am not going to the pool with you looking like that."

"I thought I looked pretty good. Am I embarrassingly fat or something?"

"I'm not talking about your weight, Mom. I'm talking about your thighs."

His eyes were darting to my thighs and then away again. What was his problem? I was getting irritated.

"What!" I said as my annoyance showed.

"Look at the inside of your thighs *Mother*."

I bent over and looked. Dear God, my pubic hair had taken over the inside of my thighs half way to my knees. How the hell had I missed that one? Shit, shit, shit! I was embarrassed in front of my kid; I was embarrassed for my kid as I wondered how long this had been going on without my knowledge.

From the looks of the mass, it was far from new and none of my friends had said a word.

So there I was standing in front of my home with my 15-year-old, and two new bushes that needed major sheering. At a time in his life I needed to show my dignity and be a good role model, what did I do?

I threw my towel at him, raced in the house, down the hall and into my bathroom squealing, "Ewwwwww".

I returned ten minutes later with a sarong on over my swimsuit.

"Well?" he said. "Did you take care of it?"

"Yes I did, but there's a bit of razor burn going on and I'm keeping the sarong until I jump in the pool. If you see any little bits of toilet paper in the pool later, don't *say anything!*"

That night I got out my 3x mirror and a spotlight. I had to be sure there were no more hair follicles on steroids. Phew!

20

Moles, Freckles and Liver Whats?

I can tell you the difference between a beauty mark and a mole. **Size!** My sister has two cute little beauty marks on her cheek. I grew up envious. My mother said I had a beauty mark on my chin.

Trust me, beauty marks do not come in golf ball size, and they don't sprout hair. I felt like the Wicked Witch of the West from the Wizard of Oz. No wonder Dorothy was afraid of her. It wasn't the broom, the teeth or the voice. It was the mole!

And as cruel as kids can be, they don't tease you over a beauty mark. I think they had every right to tease me over Big Bertha. She was a monster.

I was stuck with her so I did my best to do maintenance. Too young to own tweezers, I snuck my sister's and pulled the single hair out of Big Bertha. She bled and I didn't care. She deserved it.

After a while Bertha produced two hairs ...and then three ... and then four. By the time I was shaving my armpit forest at ten, I added shaving Bertha to my morning maintenance ritual.

It wasn't pretty. It was the fastest growing hair on the planet and I often shaved her twice a day. By the time I was 18, she would have looked like the long tail of a mullet if not carefully tended.

All those years, my mother still insisted Bertha was a beauty mark. Mothers!

At 20, Bertha's time had come. I had a job and my own medical insurance. I made an appointment with a dermatologist.

"I want to get the mole off my chin," I announced with relief.

"I wouldn't do that if I were you," he responded looking down his nose at me over his bifocals.

"So why not? I've hated it my whole life. I'm sick of it."

"Well, because it's a big one and if I take it off, you'll be left with a crater. Surely a mole looks better to you than a hole in your chin."

"Can't you just sew the hole closed?"

"Since your insurance doesn't cover cosmetic surgery, I can honestly say you'll have a scar that's less attractive than the mole."

Deflated and depressed, I took Bertha home.

If you're wondering whatever happened to her, well, she's still around. We made a truce of sorts. After 38 years and over 14,000 shaves the girl has gone pale. She started fading about the year I stopped hating her.

* * *

Other, less notorious moles, sprout on men and women all the time. There's the flat head; the dangler; the baby Bertha and the tiny little beauty mark that multiplies into freckle city.

The only moles I find ugly now that I've made peace with Bertha, are the danglers. When you talk to someone with a dangler on their neck, you tend to stare at it. You don't want to be rude. You just can't help it.

It's like talking to a female with an enormous bust. I don't care whether you're male or female, if something that huge is in front of you, you stare at it/them.

I think if the coin trick where you make it look like a quarter is coming from someone's ear could be tweaked, a quick pull off could be accomplished and no one would be the wiser. I mean those things are dangling from a thread.

As cheap as I am, I'd gladly donate the quarter.

I pulled one off my son's dog and he didn't notice. The entire family was glad to see it go.

It made me brave enough to pull one off my own neck and contrary to the stories I'd been told, I did not bleed to death.

I've also read moles can be cancerous but honestly, any mole that's dangling just trying to get away is probably not of a cancerous variety and I see no reason to make a doctor appointment; wait a month; then wait an hour in the waiting room and another thirty minutes in the exam room and then pay for removal and a biopsy.

If you've ever had moles burned off, it's no picnic. First they give you shots of Novocain or Lidocaine. Then before it numbs anything, they burn off the offending brown growths. So each spot stings twice.

By the time you get home, you have grown more which makes you wonder if someone sprinkled mole seeds on you before you left the doctor's office.

The closer I get to being a bona fide senior citizen, the more I think about having a yearly burn off as a birthday gift to myself.

I plan on becoming a senior citizen at about 84, but if there's a senior citizen discount at the dermatologist, I could lower my number temporarily.

* * *

I always wanted freckles and I finally got them. I think they're called liver spots. Who named them that? They have nothing whatsoever to do with the liver. I don't think they're even the same color as the liver.

Probably some grown disgruntled man child coined the phrase just to tick off his aging mother.

If you insist on calling them age freckles, that's fine with me. To me they are just plain freckles, and they adorn areas that were frequented by the sun.

Besides, they block the view of my arm hair and some of the wrinkles on my hands.

All the cutest girls had them, and now I do too.

21

Dumb Shit

Remember all those pictures you threw out because you didn't like how you looked? Pretty funny now isn't it? Of course there were good reasons at the time, like:
- Your hair looked stupid
- Your glasses looked stupid
- You broke up with that boyfriend
- You divorced that husband
- You thought you were fat, but that was 28 pounds ago.
- Or ...you had a fat period in your 30's only to have a fatter one in your 40's. We won't talk about the 50's except to say you wish you would have kept the 30's and 40's photos.
- Or...you finally got it together and are the perfect weight; you're in shape but you wish you had fat pictures to see how far you've come.

And who of us would have foreseen that we could have taken those old photos, copied them to our computer and Photo-Shopped them to erase the pimples;

tone down the hair or even remove the glasses. Heck, you can even make yourself thinner or give your boobs a lift.

Of course I'm not saying you *would* do that, only that you *could*. (By the way I do not make public appearances.)

As for me, I kept pictures of me in every size from a 5 to an 18 and what I notice most now is the lack of wrinkles (even though my face looks a little tight in the pudgy pics.)

Still, it is part of life… a visual journal.

So keep the pictures and a good sense of humor. Seems to me, if I think I'm wrinkled now, I better have some pictures because looking back in twenty years I'll think I'm gorgeous!

Cleanliness is next to Godliness

Look, I don't know who came up with this one but I hate it. I know women who seem to spend their entire life cleaning.

By the time their kids are grown and gone, the house looks and smells like a museum.

The worst part is, the expectation makes me feel like a failure sometimes. Everyone likes a clean house but there has to be some kind of balance.

I know for a fact, on my deathbed, I will not be saying I should have kept the house cleaner. I'm no slob (in my own mind) but I'm far from anal about "everything in its place" like husband number two was.

When I lived alone, my house was spotless because I was hardly ever there. Once I had kids it just seemed if I cleaned constantly I was going to miss their growing up. Now that they're grown, I know I made the right choice.

So why do I have lingering moments of guilt? Because

I'm a woman and should be able to do it ALL. Never mind that when I moved out with the kids, my ex called to ask me where the silverware drawer was. (It wasn't messy, he'd just never been in the kitchen.)

What Grosses Me Out

I am not afraid of mice, snakes or spiders and don't understand why anyone would be. On the other hand there is something I hate to touch and gives me the willies. Ready?

It's hair. This doesn't even make sense to *me* but I've had this stupid phobia as long as I can remember.

I love long hair. Love it! I enjoy brushing it, braiding it, wrapping it up in a bun or putting it into a ponytail. It makes me feel feminine.

But wait! I just said I hated to touch hair. Let me define my hair phobia.

The minute it is no longer ON my head (or anyone else's) it becomes icky! Yes, and a wad of the stuff taken from my hair brush, is even worse. I have been known to bag it, seal the bag and take it out to the trash so I'm sure I never have to touch it again!

Is there anything worse? Yes. Heaven forbid, if it's wet. I cannot bring myself to touch wet hair. I'll take a piece of toilet paper to get a single hair off the sink, the toilet or out of the tub so I can clean those places because the thought of hair stuck to a toilet brush or a scrubby leaves me nauseous.

I even check the shower before I get in, to be sure there are no attack hairs that might cling to me.

You have no idea how difficult it is for me to clean out the tub drain. I'd rather pack up my entire house and move to avoid confronting wet drain hair.

Mice

What I don't understand is, people who are afraid of mice. Someone tell me if this is the same thing as my hair phobia because honestly I think mice are cute.

I've never squealed or jumped on a chair, but maybe I should have done something about Fred.

After divorce #2, the kids and I were living in little house in the woods. The woods were fabulous; the house was not. Anyway, one night we were watching a movie and we noticed a little field mouse sitting on his hind legs watching us from the hall.

It was adorable. We already had cats, dogs, ferrets and chickens so what the heck. We named him Fred.

We'd see Fred every day but he was a polite little mouse. I never found Fred poop so I was happy to have him. One morning I questioned having Fred when I woke up and he was sitting on my bed watching me. That was a little disconcerting so I pointed my finger at Fred and told him that was a no-no.

I didn't see Fred for a few weeks. None of us did, but apparently he'd been a busy mouse bragging to all the girls about his new place because one morning I got up and found mouse poop in a clean bowl in the cupboard.

I was sorely disappointed when I realized Fred was a bigamist who was too busy procreating to teach his offspring any house manners. I did some serious searching in the cupboards, closets and laundry room and anywhere there was a wastebasket.

Fred was no longer cute; too many lines had been crossed; war was declared; mousetraps bought and unfortunately for the Fred clan, their 'last meal' was peanut butter (turns out they love this more than cheese).

Snakes

Snakes get a bad rap and it's not fair. Without them, families like Fred's would have taken over the world long ago. Anyway, I like them and have no problem holding them.

In fact, the kids and I have had several as pets. My two favorites were Nina the Ball Python who my son got as a youngin. She had a wonderfully sweet disposition and enjoyed being held.

Then there was Angel. The girl scared me half to death at first because she was a tad bit over nine feet long but she had been abandoned and needed rescuing. What else could I do but take care of her once I realized she had pneumonia? And once I found her weak spot, we bonded.

One day I was running water for a bath and Angel wanted out of her giant aquarium. Swaying her head near the top of her abode, my son and I took her out (she was too heavy for me alone) and she tried to fast track to the bathroom. Turned out she loved water and swam figure eights until she tired and then hung herself to dry on the towel rack. Not only did I find this adorable but it may have given me a false sense of security around snakes.

One day on a walk at the water's edge down in Georgia I saw a baby snake. "Oooh, I said, you are so cute. Let me see what kind you are."

Now the 10 inch snake was minding its own business when I started following it, but I was so curious to know what kind of snake it was that I pursued the little fellow.

All of a sudden he rose up into the striking position. Now I knew I'd scared him for him to act so huffy so I stopped a good ways out of striking distance and my mouth dropped.

Now that he was perfectly still I could see I was having a standoff with a Copperhead.

Copperheads are venomous, especially the young. They won't kill you but you will definitely need a trip to the hospital.

I backed away slowly and he lowered himself and disappeared.

I would rather face another Copperhead than clean the hair out of the shower drain.

22

Pregnancy

Looking back, pregnancy was the beginning of the aging process. First there was weight gain, stretch marks and food cravings.

I don't know about you, but while I was marveling at the growth in my belly, the rest of me was trying to stay in sync. And those stretch marks were sneaky.

First there were a few on my boobs. It wasn't really a problem because I'd been forewarned. The problem was no one told me they reproduce while you're sleeping.

One morning I woke up to find they'd spread like a rash to my belly, hips, thighs and ass. This was just the first trimester. I blame food cravings.

Can someone tell me why we don't crave raw vegetables for more than an hour? To this day, I see a box of Velveeta Cheese product and gain 22 pounds. 18 pounds of that is from water retention since salt is the first ingredient and cheese probably the last.

With my first pregnancy I actually thought it was cheese until I realized I could go surfing on my feet alone.

I haven't bought any since; figuring the 3 cases I ate in my third trimester may still be in there somewhere. I'm not sure if I'm still retaining water or I'm just fat.

I realize not everyone gains 60 pounds like I did the first time around but the affects are still the same to some degree. It's like a balloon.

The first time you blow up a balloon, it's very difficult. You pull, tug and stretch on it to get it ready and eventually you get it blown up. It's a process. If you let the air out, does it go back to the same size? Hell no.

You just stretched it out and each time you blow it up again, it gets easier. Correspondingly, each time you let the air out, it's just a tad bit bigger.

Any woman whose body appears to go back to its pre-pregnancy state was wearing a pillow and adopted on the side; owns a damn good girdle; or has a plastic surgeon in the family.

My stomach skin still looks like swag drapery. I guess I should be grateful the sag is dipped perfectly right in the middle because after 26 years, I'm guessing it's not going away by itself.

* * *

And if you had any foods you stopped eating when you were pregnant, it left a mark too.

My second pregnancy had me rushing out to the sidewalk in a full penguin waddle to upchuck sushi because the bathroom stalls were made for skinny people.

I wouldn't eat it at all now if I wasn't pushed. Guess whose favorite food it is? Yup the one who was in Hotel Mom when I got sick. The guy has been in love with sushi since he was four years old; even to the extent of choosing it over ice cream. Go figure.

Not long ago, now 24, he took me out to dinner. He ordered 4 different sushi appetizers. I ate one of each. He put his chopsticks down kind of huffy.

"Mom, I keep trying to find a sushi you like but you hardly eat any at all. In fact, I just realized I've never seen you eat much sushi. Don't you like it?"

"It's okay," I smiled. "But there's a little story I guess I never told you . . ." and I gave him the details. I love guys. You can tell them all about nausea and puking while they're eating and it doesn't faze them one bit.

We had a good laugh; he gleefully hogged the rest of the sushi; and I ordered the most awesome avocado spring rolls on the planet.

* * *

Smells don't leave the memory banks either. Remember how some normal everyday things made you nauseous? All dish soap at the store, except Joy lemon gave me the gift of gag with pregnancy number three. It still sits by my sink today ... but I swear it's a new bottle.

* * *

Okay, so pregnancy leaves telltale signs on the body. What about the mind? Those mood swings were but a glimpse of the future when menopause would kick in.

We went through the first stage of pregnancy hormones with *The Glow*. Totally harmless; we looked fabulous.

Stage two was *Food Cravings*. It only lasted the first trimester but it was fun so we kept going with that one.

Stage three was *Weepy*. We would cry over odd things with no provocation.

Stage four was *Forgetfulness* but I can't remember what I forgot or how long that lasted.

Stage five was *Post Partum Depression*. Some days it was ten times worse than all the above combined, but most the time we were too busy with the kids or imagining creative ways to off our husbands to think about it.

23

Raising Kids

If pregnancy and childbirth don't kill you, raising kids might. It's the toughest most important job on the planet. You must raise your kids to think for themselves while helping them to make intelligent choices so that they will grow into loving, honest, responsible human beings and you don't have a clue how to do it!

We are talking about on-the-job-training!

Of course this means lots of interaction instead of giving them cookies and soda and sitting them in front of the boob tube or the Nintendo. (Which I'm guessing is now Play Station or X Box.) The right way takes far more time, is incredibly frustrating, makes you wonder about 18 times a day why you chose to do this motherhood gig…until you see those little munchkins sound asleep, and your eyes fill with tears.

You can finally sit down without being interrupted.

* * *

When kids are little, you age from physical, mental and

emotional exhaustion.

Let's not forget sleep deprivation, the loss of privacy and any sex life; and teaching your toddler the dog is not a horse and the tail needs to stay attached to the cat.

Amidst all this, you have no time to get your head examined because you have faulty wiring that thinks another baby won't be any more work than the one you've got or that once you have a toddler, you've completely forgotten the birthing process and feel some cosmic pull to have another baby. Some of us are actually hard wired to think babies and toddlers are cute!

These hormonal problems are far worse than anything menopause has to offer.

By the time we come to our senses, the kids are out of those phases and we're stuck with them since they come with a no return policy.

Then one night the kids all fall asleep early and you don't.

The next morning you wake up pregnant with your first gray hair because you finally know what you got yourself into.

* * *

Just when you get used to one stage, they enter another. And it's a vicious cycle. Here's just a few:

- They get teeth
- Their teeth fall out
- They get more teeth

- They love school
- They hate school

- They love school (girlfriend/boyfriend)
- They hate school (girlfriend/boyfriend)
- They graduate anyway

- They love you
- They hate you
- They love you
- They look at you like you're an alien

- They leave toys scattered all over the floor
- They learn to pick up their toys
- They leave clothes scattered all over the floor
- You assume they pick up their clothes since they moved out because they show up at your house looking clean and unwrinkled.

- They fall in love
- They fall out of love
- They fall in love
- They get a broken heart
- They tell you that couldn't possibly know what it's like

* * *

You find it's all a cruel joke that it gets harder instead of easier. Just when you get used to them skateboarding without a helmet (meaning you found it hidden behind their bed and didn't have a coronary), they are driving a car.

Mine wouldn't wear helmets for that either.

Next thing you know, they're moving out. You have

the freedom you longed for but you don't have a clue what to do with it.

Your dreams have been on hold so long, you can't remember what they were.

You can't remember the last time you did something by yourself or for yourself so you go through all the books you've been saving.

You swear you got one called "Life after Kids for Dummies" last Christmas. Before you find it, you get sidetracked when the dog comes to say hi (he sniffs your butt) and the next thing you know you're following him around talking to him like a toddler…

"Are you hungry?"
"Do you need a walk?"
"Want to go to the store with me?"

It's pitiful but all transitions take time. In answer to your questions, the dog jumps on the sofa and licks his butt to give you a clue. You are now a pain in the ass even to the dog.

It's time to buck up and get your shit together. If you put as much time into yourself the next ten years as you did your children for the past ten years alone, you'll be in great physical health, have exuberant energy and close to ten million bucks.

This is no time to be tired or scared. This is what you worked for!

24

The Snap, Crackle and Pop of Exercise

Exercise is one of those many hindsight things. You know...woulda... coulda... shouda?

If I *woulda* exercised all along I wouldn't be going through the snap, crackle, pop of starting again in my late fifties. I would not have gotten Restless Leg Syndrome; the aches and pains would be less and I might still have my ass.

I *coulda* exercised. All the excuses were just that. Excuses! How embarrassing to realize now, that I was the L word. I hate the L word.

I *shoulda* fit it into my schedule. I knew better. Every time I felt guilty about it, I'd promise myself I'd start tomorrow.

I'm no longer queen of denial, although it was a long reign. Ten years of saying I'd start exercising tomorrow caught up with me, passed me by and laughed in my face. The 57 times I started and only exercised for a week don't count.

When I moved to Minnesota to be with my kids, my middle son kindly gave me a little talk.

"I remember as a kid not being able to keep up with you when you ran. Remember when everyone called me the Pillsbury Dough Boy?

Now I probably run six miles in the time it takes you to walk one. If you haven't noticed, we've traded places. What happened to you?"

"I got busy."

"You know that's an excuse."

"Of course it is. I've got more of them too. It all started when Izzy died. That dog was my motivational running partner. She knew the schedule. Every other day she'd stick her cold nose on my face at 6:00a.m and if I tried to hide under the covers, she'd jump on the bed and burrow under the blankets and nuzzle me 'til I got up.

Her excitement was contagious.

And then I had no one to play tennis with; the trampoline broke and I lost a wheel on my roller blades and I started working 12 to 15 hours a day.

There's more of course. I had a new one for every day the past ten years, but it doesn't matter. It's time. I'm now more afraid *not* to do it, than do it. There's too much at stake. How can I age gracefully if I look and feel like The Blob? At this point if I had the money to shop till I dropped, I'd probably drop in 22 minutes and have to come home and shop online."

"Okay, where do you want to start? I'll go with you for awhile."

* * *

Bless my son. It wasn't easy. We started with tennis. I was breathless after five minutes so there was a lot of stopping, starting and stretching after that. An old sensation crept into my body. What was it?

Good grief! There was oxygen entering my lungs. It had been so long I swear I could *feel* the blood circulating in my arms and legs. To top it off, my brain reacted like someone had stuck smelling salts under my nose.

What a rush!

Two days later, we went back and I remembered what muscles were. And I remembered how they speak. My thighs were whining and grumbling. Did I listen? Heck no. I was too excited at the prospect of exchanging *frumpy and dumpy* for *fit and fabulous*.

I was thinking, "No pain, no gain," as I walked with perfect posture to my side of the tennis court. I was entering a new era in my life.

I got in position to start the game with that slight squat, so you can take off in any direction to get to the ball.

Since I hadn't listened to the whining and grumbling, my thighs made a bigger statement. They froze in place when I squatted and I watched two balls wiz past me.

I stretched my legs a few minutes and tried again. This time I couldn't lift the racquet. Either someone had put weights in the handle or my arm muscles had atrophied. My arm quivered and shook when I lifted it.

Hoping my kid had played a joke on me, I checked for the weight by holding the racquet in my other hand. Shit.

Apparently that restless leg syndrome had just moved to my arm.

I stared at my arm. It was an alien! Someone had turned my arm into Jello. At least they'd used the mold of something arm-ish. Obviously I'd gone too many years without owning a mirror.

Watching the saggy arm flap blow back and forth in

the breeze, I smiled at my patient son and offered, "Maybe we should take up skydiving instead of tennis. With these wings I could fly down without a parachute."

While I was busy making a mental note to wear long sleeves until I could get my wings down to the size of a flying squirrel, my son interjected, "Stretch some more Ma, then we'll take it slow."

My boy knew how sore I was and suggested we try other things to use different muscles. Of course he was right. Alternating was good, especially after I twisted my knee during a faulty pivot.

***

I knew the only way I was going to change my life and my now wimpy body, was to make it work every single day. It had to be a habit. I didn't have to work her hard every day. I just had to make sure I got her moving.

And I needed to pay attention to her. There is a difference between no pain, no gain and abuse. Since she'd been a fluff ball for quite a while, I had to be a better listener. She was claiming abuse at every turn so I had to baby her. But first she had to remind me one more time.

* * *

She did it while running. I never loved running, just how I felt afterward. Plus I could eat a boatload, not gain weight and practically no body parts flapped in the breeze.

What I said in the *legs* chapter was true, but I pushed her pretty hard. The plan was two miles. I knew I couldn't run that far but I had to see what we could do, my body and I.

We had been speed walking on the treadmill a week.

She and I walked to warm up. We stretched a long five minutes. While she enjoyed the stretching, I was getting bored.

My son and I took off side by side. It was great. I kept the pace for close to a minute; unless it was thirty seconds. Heck, it could have been twenty seconds. I was busy trying to remember how to breathe and I'd look like an idiot if I checked my watch so soon.

She asked to stop and I told her no, but I slowed down so she could breathe a little easier and we watched my kid move ahead of us.

"See you on the next round," I heard him say as he left his mother in the dust.

As an incline approached, I yelled, "You can do it!" in my mind since I was too out of breath to say it out loud.

She did it! When she asked to stop at the top, I begged her to just run as far as the next picnic table and she made it. We walked a bit. Hopefully I looked better than I felt.

I had a mental picture of a cartoon character crossing the desert hunched over with arms, head and tongue hanging. The buzzards were circling.

We alternated walking and running (which was really a jog but running sounds so much better).

There were hills at that park I could barely walk, let alone run and after the first mile loop I knew I'd run her as far as she was going to go. But still I pushed. I asked her for one more mile just to walk. We needed to keep up our heart rate to help shrink those wings and slapping thunder thighs.

She wasn't thrilled but she was determined to please me. She didn't want to disappoint our son either.

Our performance wasn't quite stellar but considering her condition, we felt pretty good, except for the knee that missed the follow-through on the pivot during tennis.

The high impact of running had done a number on her. She was throbbing.

I kept my mouth shut about it for a few days. I wrapped it and walked the treadmill.

"You know you need to let it heal," my kid said to me.

"But I don't want to lose momentum."

"And you don't want a permanent injury."

"Honey, I'm running out of time! I'm 58 years old for God's sake."

"Ma, you're 57."

"Oh, thank God. I'll take a week off," and then we picked a movie from Netflix and settled on the sofa.

* * *

After a week, the knee was not much better so I stuck to the treadmill and did some free weights. Thank god they come in a one pound size because lifting my hands above my head was tough enough. I wondered if I could do more than six lifts if I used just a single one pound weight for both hands and cut my fingernails to lighten the load.

When I tried to do a pull-up, I couldn't pull up. I couldn't even hang on to the bar. The weight of my dangling body was more than I could cope with. I never considered myself strong, but this was ridiculous. I had turned into a cupcake.

Next I started jumping on the trampoline. That should be easy right? I snuck out early in the morning when the sun came up so I could avoid the neighbors. I knew I didn't have to jump high. I could work up to it.

The biggest challenge was how to get on the thing. My arm wings were useless. They wouldn't fly me up there and I had no muscle under them to pull myself up the traditional way. I had to improvise.

I looked to the left; I looked to the right. I had to scan my surroundings to be sure there were no witnesses. Carefully I put my leg up on the trampoline and followed it with my chest and did a scooting motion not unlike a toddler. Admittedly, a toddler looks svelter.

Once that hurdle was accomplished I sat in the middle of it and thought of all the things that could go wrong and how I could fall off it and break something.

Then I had a good laugh at me. After my second divorce I had worked hard at being the best I could be. I attended a Tony Robbins weekend where I did the fire walk.

How could I, a woman who'd walked barefoot across 2,000 degree red hot coals totally unscathed, be afraid of falling off a great big trampoline?

When had I lost me again? I sat in a half lotus position (well as close as I could get to it) and closed my eyes and remembered the real me. Determined, I stood up and started jumping. It took a few minutes to figure out how to do it without my knee hurting, but I did it.

Next thing you know I was chanting, "All I need is within me now." If you've ever read or watched Tony Robbins, you'll get that. Or if you've watched *'The Secret'* or any other of the wonderful folks out there that remind us *thoughts become things.)*

Anyway, I started feeling stronger and stronger; except my boobs hurt. Apparently I needed an iron bra but I didn't have one and didn't want to ruin the moment so I looked to the left; looked to the right and scanned my surroundings to be sure there were no witnesses and held on to the girls with my hands. Heck, it worked. They weren't going anywhere and it gave my arms something to do.

I jumped and jumped. I felt totally alive and smiled at the birds, the trees and the rising sun. I saw a turkey hen lead her three babies across the yard and I felt totally blessed and filled with gratitude.

Thirty minutes later I was ready to start my day with an oxygenated body in a state filled with gratitude. I slowed down and then stopped my jumping. I stretched a few minutes and got off the trampoline the same way I got on.

As my feet touched the earth, I was acutely aware my legs had turned to rubber. My knees wobbled and I fought the feeling of greeting Mother Earth with my kneecaps. Cursing that I felt like Gumby I was also grateful I wasn't wobbling on all fours like his sidekick Pokey.

I decided to celebrate with a cup of coffee and a cigarette.

* * *

My daughter was feeling left out of the "help Mom exercise" campaign, plus she was a little ticked off I'd run farther than she had.

Insisting that running was not her forte, she suggested we go bicycle riding. I laughed.

"What's so funny?"

"Have you ever seen me ride a bike?" I asked her.

"No, I've just seen you Rollerblade, why?"

"I've never had a bicycle of my own. Other kids in my neighborhood let me ride theirs but it's been awhile."

"How long has it been?"

I thought; and realized I sometimes hate math. "Well, Darlin', just about 50 years, so I think we should do it."

"Yeah! I'll get the bikes and bring them over. We'll go to the park and ride six miles."

Was I fearful? Let's just say if I had knee pads, elbow pads and a helmet, and any other pad, I would have worn them. Turned out getting the bikes in and out of my car was the hardest part.

I was nervous too.

"Oh Mom, you'll be fine. I'll stay with you."

"No! Don't get too close or I might mow you down. I have no idea how this is going to go, and if you end up looking like road kill, I'll have nightmares for the rest of my life."

I continued, "I know I can do it, I'm just not sure how long it will take. Now show me how to use the hand brakes. The bikes I rode all had foot brakes and I'd hate to dismount over the handlebars."

After instructions, we took off. I followed her and I completely missed the path. I bumped across the grass like a five year old with her very first bicycle wishing someone would put the training wheels back on.

I stayed upright because I was too afraid to fall.

The first thing I noticed was there wasn't much of a seat on the thing. After a ½ mile of squiggling back and forth on the path and thanking my lucky stars there wasn't anyone to mow down with my bicycle ineptitude, I straightened out and got used to it.

As soon as I was riding in a relatively straight line I wondered if part of the problem wasn't the seat. I was beginning to feel molested. The skinny seat was trying to go where few men have gone before and it wasn't being very diplomatic about it either.

After a mile my thighs were burning, and I do mean burning. The thought of rubbing two sticks together to start a fire preceded thoughts of spontaneous combustion.

How could they look like the same old legs when they felt like a deep fried turkey still cooking at an internal temperature of 425 degrees?

My bright idea daughter asked how I was doing. Since she was a girl, and my daughter, I told her the truth. My answer was crass.

She had the audacity to laugh at me. Then she spewed, "I know it hurts, that's why you need to ride like I do. Just stand up and peddle!" and she took off like a big fat know-it-all.

Since her back was facing me I wholeheartedly gave her the finger. I felt better and she'd never know.

I tried standing to ride. An inch off the seat, I was out of control so I went back to the molestation process.

I stopped and took off my sweatshirt, wadded it up and put it between my butt and the seat, but that seat was a professional. No sweatshirt could stop it.

At the next hill my thighs made a comment. If they had their own fingers, they would have displayed the middle one for me so I got off the bicycle and walked.

Where was a cab when you needed one?

After two miles, my kid was ready to quit. I tried to act disappointed but I'm sure I didn't pull it off. I wasn't capable of walking correctly. I would have looked better if I'd just finished a 20 mile horseback ride. At least my bowed legs made it impossible for my thighs to clap in approval at wrestling that two wheeled demon into the car.

The next time the two of us rode the trails, I stuck a couple hand towels down my pants to protect my cheeks and you-know-who. I hid in the car till there was no one in site, then made a dash to get the bikes out and me on my designated vehicle before anyone could see I looked like I was wearing two extra thick depends adult diapers.

They didn't help and I'm not riding again until we can get non x-rated seats. If I want to have sex with an inanimate object, I'll do it in the privacy of my own home.

* * *

Longing for something easier, I decided walking was a fabulous idea. Besides, my 13-year-old dog needed exercise too. It was something we could do every day. I had fantasies of these long, quiet, bonding walks on the park trails absorbing the beauty of nature to my very soul.

And who better to do it with than my dog? Now there's a partner who won't talk your ear off.

What I got was a dog who thought I was taking him out on maneuvers. Every person, dog, duck, squirrel, bird or passing car (if we were near the entrance) was a threat and he let them know about it, while I tugged, pulled and apologized.

The first dozen times were not relaxing in any way shape or form. A quarter mile left me a frazzled, emotional wreck.

Still, it was MY fault he'd never been out in public and that he was a total pain in the ass.

Then my know-it-all son brought something to my attention. This is where raising your kids and teaching them everything you know has a downside. If they listen, they pass you up, leave you in the dust, and then are able to teach you if you can keep your ego from spewing unnecessary words that make you look even dumber.

I admit it's fascinating to be mad and proud at the same time. The bottom line with the dog? I was so afraid of him being 'bad'...he was! I'd see a squirrel at 50 yards and tighten the leash in preparation; a clear signal for him there was something nearby to chase, so he did.

Still I pressed on. We both deserved it. In a short, uh, eight months we began having the walks of my dreams.

Those quarter mile walks grew to quick paced two mile walks. We enjoyed the trees, a lovely duck inhabited pond and a bridge over a cattail filled marsh with noisy songbirds and busy squirrels.

When he saw people, he was sure they wanted to shower him with affection so we still had some adjusting to do there but it was doable.

All was well. I was getting stronger, losing more weight (and texture) and my legs quit complaining about hills and valleys.

Then winter hit. For a girl born and raised in the San Francisco Bay Area and then spending 25 years in Georgia; Minnesota is unfathomably cold; but I was hooked on my walks and so was my dog.

I layered and still had to run to keep my hands from freezing through my gloves. With temperatures in the teens, my canine refused a jacket and had little problem with the cold.

We walked in the snow and found a different kind of peace ...until it dropped below zero and the snow turned to ice so we couldn't walk at all. Now he sits by my side expectantly while I work at the computer and we look out the window and wait for Spring.

What I've Learned from the Past

The cold gave me time to ponder and my knee a little more time to heal. I started thinking about how everything is supposed to be harder when you get older. I found myself asking a question.

"Who says?" and I couldn't answer it. I thought back over my life and times I'd been hurt and I came to a wonderfully shocking conclusion.

Remember the saying, "If you don't use it, you lose it?" I think that's more appropriate and what I'm going to stick with. From here on out, I'm giving my body the gift of exercise.

* * *

When I was 23, I did an unforgettable stretch. I hadn't done any exercise probably since I graduated from high school. Remembering how I used to literally throw my leg up on the table and stretch my face to my knee, I decided a good stretch was called for.

As I whipped my leg up onto the table I *heard* the tendons tearing. They didn't feel great either. It took six months to heal enough to not hurt when I walked and a three more to be able to exercise without pain. I remember wishing I'd broken the bone instead because I imagined it being less painful.

* * *

It's been 25 years since I threw my back out during another non-exercise period. Minding my own business, I sneezed getting out of bed ....

Why did I ever laugh at those TV sitcoms when people walked bent over? I thought it was a joke until *the sneeze*.

It was first thing in the morning. It hurt so bad I was afraid to sit down, but I couldn't stand straight either. Naturally I felt a strong need to wee in the commode.

I thought it took all I had to get to the toilet. This was not shuffling off to Buffalo. Bent awkwardly with my face facing the floor, it looked like I was keeping my eye on my opponent in a relay race and the opponent was an ant who had the lead.

Finally arriving at my destination, I couldn't for the life of me, figure how to sit! Since the choice was to sit or pee down my leg, tears filled my eyes as I lowered my bum. Reaching the toilet paper took another herculean effort and getting up may have been worse of all.

I ended up on pain pills from Doc in the Box, but it was before I'd learned about chiropractors or natural medicine.

* * *

So here I am. I've worked at a snail's pace for the last eight months to dethrone myself of my cottage cheese queen status and it seems to be working.

Exercise actually releases (or produces) growth hormone. Growth hormone grows muscle to replace some of that cottage cheese so you don't look like the aging dairy queen and it helps with collagen production as well so it slows down the wrinkle process as well.

If someone would have told me this at 20, it wouldn't have made any difference. I thought I had forever before I would get old, plus the only cottage cheese I knew about was the stuff I mixed with canned pears and I'd thought collagen was a new kind of light bulb.

Live and learn. That's what I like best about life.

25

The Highs and Lows, Hot and Colds of Menopause

I'll tell you why they call it menopause, because the new balance of hormones makes you grow hair like a man! Your husband gets your boobs, and you get his mustache. Swell.

Let's just say I wasn't looking forward to the adventure.

First, I didn't believe my natural practitioner when she told me I was going through menopause. I was in my mid forties. I had a seven year old and I didn't even feel middle aged yet. Was she crazy or was I simply frightened?

The truth is, I was terrified. It would be the end of being a woman.

I told her I wasn't going through it because I still had my period and everything was normal. No hot flashes, no mood swings and I still loved sex.

She just smiled and said, "There are a lot of other

changes going on Andrea. They are subtle and they take years. I just want you to know there are herbs you can take to help keep things balanced if you start feeling off kilter."

A year or so later, as she predicted, I started having a few cranky moments and my body temperature felt like it went up and down faster than a yoyo. She gave me some herbs to balance me out.

That was fine and dandy until I found out that caffeine brings on hot flashes. No more coffee on a summer morning. No more Pepsi in the afternoon. My first summer, I cut back on both those things to stop from being sweat drenched before 8 am. Life was not fair.

Winter arrived and I learned the power of hot flashes. My job at the time was cleaning new construction homes, inside and out, every window, nook and cranny without any heat. I know it wasn't good for me but how could I resist?

Four cups of coffee and I could be outdoors in 35 degrees on an extension ladder scraping paint from second story windows in a t-shirt!

A Pepsi with my lunch salad and I was set for the afternoon. That was the shit. Never mind I was wearing out my adrenal glands. All my life I'd been the first one to get cold. Now I felt unstoppable. It was awesome.

… Until I got home from work and my husband had the thermostat cranked up to 70 degrees. I'd put on a tank top and take frequent trips to the back yard to cool myself down.

In a few short years, my period stopped, the hot flashes were non-existent (unless I overdid the caffeine) and I found out what menopause was really about.

It's about FREEDOM.

You don't have to mess with having a period. You don't have to worry about getting pregnant; and you can, uh, fool around whenever you want! Awesome stuff!

The fact of the matter is, I don't feel old. I feel younger, until I catch a glimpse of those wrinkles. No stage in life is perfect.

Here's a conversation which took place between my daughter and I a year after I stopped menstruating.

"Oh god Mom, I just started my period. I am so SICK of this shit. I feel like I live in the bathroom. I'm constantly checking for leaks. I think I feel one, rush to the bathroom and nothing. Other times I don't notice and someone at work points. You have no idea embarrassing that is!"

I gave her the Mom look. "You're right! I have no idea what it's like."

Ignoring me she went on. "Plus it seems like everyone on earth can tell when I'm on my period. How the hell can they tell?"

I tilted my head and asked, "Could it be the mood swings?"

"What do you mean...mood swings!?!? Oh well, that *could* have something to do with it I guess. Am I really that moody?"

I smiled, "Darlin', you're wearing a neon sign."

"Oh." She looked down and sighed. "Was it this bad for you?"

"Yup! It's never fun but you get used to it, because you have to."

"Mom, I just want it to stop."

"Honey, how long have you had your period?"

"It's been four years!"

Mentally, I drop to the floor; roll back and forth twice,

kick my feet a few times and slap the floor with my left hand repeatedly.

"Honey, when you've had the damn thing for 20 years, you can whine a little. When you have a month long period after having a baby, you can be annoyed as hell. When you've had it 40 years you can complain all you want; but not yet.

I smiled, "By the way, I don't have any tampons."

"But..." she starts in and I interrupt her.

"No pads either. I don't get cramps. I don't have mood swings or breakouts. I can wear white pants if I want; I don't ruin my underwear and I don't have to change my sheets repeatedly one week out of the month ...because I don't have a period anymore."

I give her a great big grin and continue, "I threw out the last of the tampons because you weren't here and I never want to see one again. I am a free and happy woman and life is wonderful."

I detected a hint of jealousy so I added, "Did I get carried away with that?"

"Yes, Mother. You did."

"Oh honey, I'm so *NOT* sorry!"

I did the booty dance and laughed uproariously.

26

Am I Grown Up Yet?

I'm beginning to think I'll never feel grown up and I think I finally figured out why.

I'm going to get a little philosophical here. Let's look at plants. They're either growing or dying. They don't just grow up and say, "Hey, glad I'm done with that shit. Whew, what a chore. Now I'm just going to sit here and do nothing."

It's like us getting to a certain age and retiring. Hello? What does the word *retire* mean? Are we supposed to lie down? How boring is that?

What do plants really do? They grow or they die. There's always at least a subtle change going on.

Where I used to feel some disappointment in the fact that I can't just sit around, relax and do nothing; it also makes perfect sense. If I wasn't learning something new, if I wasn't *doing* anything, I'd probably die from boredom!

It turns out that true and lasting happiness is quite simply this: Growing!

If I am growing, and giving, I am happy. When I feel I

am moving forward in life, either personally, professionally, emotionally or spiritually, I can't wait to get up in the morning. It is only in stagnation that I wilt like a flower.

We just weren't made to sit around and do nothing. Growing is awesome.

If I could go back to a time when I had no wrinkles... I wouldn't do it! I wouldn't do it because I don't ever want to lose what I've learned. Heaven knows I don't want to have to learn this stuff again. It was tough enough the first time.

I've loved and lost; loved and lost; (you get the picture here) but the important truth is, everyone who enters our life is a gift whether we choose to see it that way or not. Everyone teaches us something.

They may teach us what to do or what not to do, but at the end of the day, it's what we do with the lessons we've learned that count.

And there are always people who love us, even when we're feeling sorry for ourselves and think otherwise. It's a crazy world and laughter makes it work.

Growing in this case, means learning. The more you learn, the more you realize you don't know!

And who has time to feel old when they're busy learning more stuff?

Not me!

ABOUT THE AUTHOR

Andrea lives in Minnesota where even hot flashes can't keep her warm in the winter.

Made in the USA
Lexington, KY
27 July 2016